KT-599-987

Berlitz®

Switzerland

Front cover: A traditional
Swiss chalet in the Alps

Right: St Bernard mountain
rescue dog

TOP 10 ATTRACTIONS

The Matterhorn • A constant challenge to mountaineers from around the world *(page 99)*

Engadine • Zernez is the main gateway to the Swiss National Park *(page 80)*

Basel Carnival •
This popular three-day cultural event takes place during Lent *(page 38)*

Lucerne and its lake •
At the heart of William Tell country *(page 64)*

The Jet d'Eau The tallest monument in Geneva reaches the height of a 40-storey building *(page 103)*

Château de Chillon Austerely beautiful, the old stronghold of Château de Chillon looks out over Lake Geneva *(page 118)*

Bern The capital is listed by UNESCO as one of the world's cultural treasures *(page 46)*

The Bernese Oberland This spectacular region of mountains, lakes and glaciers works a special magic on visitors *(page 56)*

Zillis Where the oldest painted ceiling in Europe can be seen *(page 80)*

Ticino Its valleys and lakes have an Italian feel *(page 84)*

CONTENTS

70

123

98

61

35

53

INTRODUCTION

A country of contrasts and of great natural and cultural resources, Switzerland is going through a period of important changes. At the start of the 21st century, past and future coexist, confronting and complementing each other in a present that many Swiss see as less perfect than that of a few years ago, with the hint of further socio-political changes to come.

In this small country at the heart of old Europe, larch trees climb the mountainsides of the Alps, whose peaks are cloaked in eternal snows; fierce torrents hurl their icy waters into mirrored lakes; verdant valleys resonate with the tinkling of heavy bells hung from the necks of plump, well-kept cows. Here and there, a castle gives the landscape a fairy-tale look. And everywhere, during the summer, geraniums cascade from windows and balconies.

The Eiger, Mönch and Jungfrau

No map can recreate the geographic reality of Switzerland. Nearly two-thirds of the country is mountainous. Some summits are more than 4,500m (14,750ft) high; no one can resist the myths surrounding the Matterhorn (Mont Cervin) or the imposing trio formed by the Eiger, the Mönch and the Jungfrau. To the east, beneath the slopes of the Grisons, lie the prestigious ski slopes of Arosa, Davos and St Moritz. Fertile lowlands, situated between the Alps to the southeast and the rocky green range of

The Glacier Express on the Landwasser viaduct in the Grisons the Jura to the northeast, spread in a circle between Lake Geneva and Lake Constance. At once pastoral and industrialised, this narrow band contains all the big cities and the majority of the 7.5 million inhabitants that make up the Confederation.

The diversity of Switzerland, however, goes beyond its landscape and climate, which is Alpine in the mountainous regions and nearly Mediterranean in southernmost Ticino. Cultural currents converge at this linguistic crossroads wedged between powerful neighbours. Three major languages have official status: in fact, some 65 percent of the population speaks *Schwyzerdütsch*, an Alemannic German dialect, while 19 percent claims French as their major language, and 10 percent Italian. A fourth national language, Romansh (1 percent), spoken in some Grisons mountain valleys, owes its survival to the fierce determination of its speakers. Each group has its own traditions, literature, gastronomy and way of life, but there are cultural interchanges – some of them institutional, others more hidden, none of them easy – that make Switzerland a vibrant patchwork of individuals and ideas.

Grass-roots Government

Politically, a grass-roots democratic system takes account of regional aspirations. Each of the 26 cantons and demi-cantons that make up Switzerland enjoys considerable autonomy, as do some 3,000 communes, both rural and urban. Popular initiatives and referenda are used on the local and national level to propose new laws or to abolish contested regulations. All of these mechanisms make the political apparatus somewhat cumbersome, slowing the decision-making process.

As Switzerland has chosen to have a grass-roots parliament, so it has also chosen to have a grass-roots, militia-based army: all eligible men under the age of 42 are enrolled in the army and required to do regular military service. For, strange as it seems, neutral, peaceable Switzerland is ready to respond to any attack: anti-tank traps, bunkers and landing strips are hidden in the most bucolic valleys.

Executive power in Switzerland is entrusted to a cabinet of seven wise men and women, elected by the Parliament, in a system that respects the subtle balance of power among political parties, as well as among regions. These seven take it in turn to be President of the Confederation. Since each president's term only lasts one year, the average citizen often has a hard time remembering who is in office.

The modesty that characterises Switzerland's political figures extends to the population at large. The Swiss do not like

Dividing the cheese ceremony, Justis valley, Bernese Oberland to hear praise, either of their country's riches or of its position. Nonetheless, the average standard of living is high – and one must remember that this prosperity has been acquired in spite of meagre natural resources. Lacking coal and oil, the Swiss have struggled to tame the waters of their own Alps. Mineral resources are imported, then transformed into luxury goods that can be exported for profit.

Of course, Swiss trains are more punctual than most; of course, the pavements are cleaner and traffic laws more respected than in some neighbouring countries. But if the concern for order and detail still characterises Swiss life to an extent that may at times seem pedantic, there are also bursts of whimsy and exuberance, especially in cultural and artistic life. Also, because of the significant numbers of foreigners in the country – political refugees, immigrant workers or stars escaping the tax laws of their own countries – some neighbourhoods, particularly in the big cities, are nothing like the Swiss clichés.

City and Country

The German-speaking majority occupies most of the country, except for the west and southwest. Zurich, the economic and financial capital, is at the heart of this majority. In the realm of international finance, the 'Zurich gnomes' have the reputation of being able to make judgments that can make or break a business, or several. But for tourists, the city offers elegant boutiques, museums, music and memories of a rich past. Geneva, the largest French-speaking city, has a very cosmopolitan air, thanks to its location at the French border and the presence of dozens of international businesses and organisations there. The political capital of the Swiss Confederation, Bern, is provincial and modest, lying halfway between these two linguistic poles and economic rivals. No grand monuments or majestic avenues

A paddle steamer cruises Lake Brienz

here: Bern is too Swiss for such pomp. Nonetheless, it is one of the most agreeable capitals in Europe.

Each Swiss city has its own particular atmosphere, tied to its history, language and vocation. Even the smaller towns have much to offer culturally. One morning in a car is enough to go from the covered bridges of Lucerne to the orange groves of Lugano in the heart of the Italian region, but the spectacular change in language, culture and climate is as great as the Alps, which separate these two regions. Many Swiss villages deserve a stopover. Local arts and crafts, architecture (some small towns have remarkable medieval houses), local costumes – all offer something of interest, as does the landscape itself.

Unless you have made the trip just to visit museums and old country churches, you'll probably spend plenty of time outside, breathing the pure air of the mountains. Do you have energy to spare? Then scale the peaks or explore them

Tobogganing in Valais

on horseback; ski, windsurf (all year round), play tennis or golf; swim; go sailing, hang-gliding, waterskiing or fishing. Take a stroll in the woods or the countryside, following the yellow arrows to footpaths. Take advantage of the many mountain-bike paths throughout the country.

And the shopping… Shop windows tempt you with the most seductive luxury goods – watches, jewellery and the latest fashions. Given the quality of Swiss workmanship, these buys are worth considering. If your budget is tight, window-shop. Take time to stroll through the stalls of an open-air market; these are held once or twice a week in nearly every city and town, and you'll find flowers, fruit and vegetables in season, country bread and handmade objects.

In Switzerland you can eat well and with great variety, and there is something to suit every budget. The Geneva region, among others, is known for its extraordinary number of fine restaurants. Cheese is a favourite everywhere, in *raclettes* or fondues. Some regions, such as Valais, Neuchâtel or Ticino, are known for their wine-growing traditions. You can take a seat in the first café you see and try the local wine. No hurry: the locals spend hours there, before a *deci* (decilitre, or one-tenth of a litre) or a *demi* (half litre) of white wine, reading the newspaper.

A BRIEF HISTORY

Thousands of years before William Tell *(see page 14)*, Switzerland was covered in glaciers. Its first-known inhabitants lived in caves, eking out a living by hunting and gathering. When the glaciers receded some 5,000 years ago, the people were able to move to the banks of lakes and rivers, where they built villages on pilings.

During the Second Iron Age, somewhere around 400BC, a Celtic tribe known as the Helvetians, from whom Switzerland derives its original name, arrived in the region. In 58BC, this tribe, looking for new territory, burned their farms and encampments and emigrated to the southwest. They are estimated to have numbered about 370,000 at that time. However, the legions of Julius Caesar stopped them at Bibracte, pushed them back and colonised their territory. The Romans established their administrative capital at Aventicum, nowadays just a village (Avenches) between Lausanne and Bern.

The Romans built roads and also brought in their technical developments and culture, just as later they would be the vehicle of the new Christian religion. During the decline of the Roman Empire, the eastern half of the country fell into the hands of the Alemanni, a warlike Germanic tribe, while the west came under the control of the Burgundians. The Sarine River, which marks the boundary between these two zones, remains to this day the linguistic and cultural frontier between German- and French-speaking Switzerland.

The Middle Ages

Both the Burgundians and the Alemanni were soon succeeded by the Franks, one of the most powerful Germanic tribes. Under Charlemagne (AD768–814), the whole of what we now know as Switzerland was integrated into the Germanic Holy

Roman Empire. The abbeys that were to become centres of study and culture date from this era.

After the fall of the Carolingians in 911, a long period of political intrigue began, dominated by the powerful Zähringen and Habsburg families. In the mid-13th century, two powers emerged: the house of Savoy and the house of Habsburg. The inhabitants of central Switzerland opposed the extension of Habsburg influence, leading them to swear to a mutual assistance pact linking three valley communities, the *Waldstätten*: Uri, Schwyz and Unterwalden. This 'pact of defensive alliance', agreed upon at the beginning of August 1291, is considered to be the foundation of the Swiss Confederation, an

The William Tell Affair

In a country without kings, it is the people who make history. Whether he is based on a legend or a real person, William Tell nevertheless remains the Swiss national hero.

At the beginning of the 14th century, this simple peasant had the courage to stand up to a tyrannical governor. Having refused, in his passage through Altdorf, to salute the Bailiff Gessler, a representative of the Habsburgs, William Tell was condemned by Gessler to shoot an apple off his son's head with an arrow.

Tell succeeded in one try; when asked why he had taken two arrows from his quiver, he explained that the second was for Gessler, in case he missed his shot. Furious, the governor ordered him thrown in prison. Then, as he was being taken by boat to the castle dungeon, a storm hit the lake, the Vierwaldstättersee. Only Tell was able to keep the boat from wrecking. He was untied and brought the boat ashore at a place now known as Tellsplatte, from which he managed to escape. Later, he led an ambush against the tyrant near Küssnacht and killed him.

Friedrich Schiller's play *William Tell* runs every summer to full houses in the open-air theatres of Interlaken and Altdorf.

event commemorated every
1 August, Switzerland's national holiday. The legend of
William Tell *(see left)* dates
from around this period.

It was not until 1315 that
the alliance took on its
current meaning, when the
Waldstätten fought the Habsburgs at the battle of Morgarten. The inhabitants of
Schwyz fought so valiantly
that the whole Confederation
came to be called the 'Swiss'.
During the 14th century,

Inside the William Tell chapel

thanks to further alliances
with other communities (Lucerne, Zurich, Glarus, Zug and
Bern), the Confederation grew to eight cantons, all determined
to fight foreign aggression.

The courage and prowess of the Swiss soldiers in the battles of Sempach (1386) and Näfels (1388), where they crushed
the Habsburgs, contributed to forging a solid Swiss military
reputation. This reputation was confirmed in the Burgundian
wars (Grandson and Murten in 1476, Nancy in 1477).

Turn of the Tide

The Battle of Marignano, in 1515, marked the first defeat of
the Swiss army; more than 12,000 soldiers died in the battle.
The Confederates nonetheless preserved their military reputation, henceforth serving as mercenaries to foreign armies.
They no longer waged war on their own enemies, but rather
on those of whoever paid them. The sight alone of these powerful halberdiers had a strong effect on their adversaries. It is
their descendants who, today, stand guard at the Vatican in

Renaissance costume. In 1516 the Confederation, which by then included 13 cantons (Fribourg, Solothurn, Basel, Schaffhausen and Appenzell had joined the alliance by this time), signed a perpetual peace treaty with France. Switzerland kept its territorial acquisitions (such as Ticino), while France won the right to requisition its mercenaries at any time.

Religious Strife

The continual tensions of the 16th century were exacerbated by the Reformation. In 1522, five years after Martin Luther nailed his 95 theses to the Wittenberg church door in Germany, Ulrich Zwingli, a priest from Glarus who had become the

Ulrich Zwingli

preacher at the main church in Zurich, also defied papal authority. In the years to follow, Zurich, Bern, Basel and Schaffhausen would back the Reformation. But in the cantons of Uri, Schwyz, Unterwald, Lucerne and Zug, as well as in Solothurn and Fribourg, Catholicism remained firmly entrenched. Divided by religious zeal, the Confederation began to tear itself apart (the civil war of Kappel in 1531) before finally finding a compromise.

Through the mediation of the French reformer Guillaume Farel, Bern encouraged the propagation of the Protestant Reformation in Neu-châtel and Geneva, and took advantage of its success to spread its influence further. Under constant threat from the Duke of Savoy, Geneva called on troops from Bern to defend itself. After chasing out the Savoyards, Bern occupied Vaud, where it worked to establish the new faith. But Geneva would not be dominated. In 1541, however, another French reformer, Jean Calvin, managed to establish a Protestant theocracy in Geneva. The 'Protestant Rome' was born.

Jean Calvin

Lacking a centralised power and plagued by religious rivalries, the Confederates could not follow a coherent foreign policy. Since Marignano, they no longer participated in European conflicts except through their mercenaries. The Confederation embarked on the path of neutrality – an armed neutrality, born of the violation of Helvetian territory during the Thirty Years' War (1618–48). From 1647, this federal army, with Catholics and Protestants fighting side by side, watched over Swiss neutrality. Once peace was re-established in the treaty of Westphalia (1648), the Confederation was considered a sovereign state, its independence universally recognised. The canton of Bern played the most significant role.

From 1685 the country became a land of asylum for many French Protestants fleeing their homeland after the Revocation of the Edict of Nantes. But religious conflicts also raged in Switzerland throughout the 17th century. They broke out in 1656 (when victory went to the Catholics) and in 1712 (when the Protestants won the day), before ending in the

Aarau peace agreement, which pronounced both religions equal. In the same period, social upheavals shook a Confederation where political rights still belonged only to the privileged. The profits of banking and commerce (in cotton, silk, wool and clock-making) remained in the hands of these few.

It is not surprising, then, that the repercussions of the French Revolution of 1789 were strongly felt in Switzerland. After having occupied or annexed the portions of the Confederation they wanted (in particular Basel, the canton of Vaud, Valais, and Geneva), the revolutionary armies of France imposed the new Helvetic Republic, whose artificial, centralised structures were anathema to most Swiss citizens.

Napoleon Bonaparte put an end to three years of anarchy when he gave Switzerland a new constitution, the Act of Mediation (1803), inspired by the constitution of the ancient

A 19th-century cartoon representing the campaign for proportional representation

Confederation, and added six new cantons to the 13 existing ones. He also took conscripts with him: 8,000 Swiss men died during the retreat of Napoleon's army from Russia.

Neutral but Caring

The Congress of Vienna (1815) confirmed the independence and neutrality of Switzerland. Three new cantons (Valais, Geneva, which had been occupied by the French from 1798 to 1813, and Neuchâtel, which remained simultaneously under allegiance to Prussia until 1857) had just entered into the Confederation, giving the country its current geographic shape. But the religious struggles between Catholics and Protestants were reignited. In 1847, the Catholic cantons separated from the Confederation (the Sonderbund alliance); however, a campaign capably led by General Dufour ended three weeks later in the dissolution of the pact and imposed the return to peace. Political stability and national unity were assured in 1848 by a new constitution that established a true Swiss democracy, with power shared equally among communal, canton and federal authorities. The 1874 Constitution is still in effect today, and has preserved these foundations.

Internationally, Switzerland has been recognised since 1863, when Henri Dunant founded the Red Cross in Geneva. Since then, the country has offered asylum to many important refugees, from Lenin to Solzhenitsyn.

Geneva, headquarters of the League of Nations from 1920, has since become the European seat of the United Nations. Paradoxically, until 2002, Switzerland chose to remain outside the UN, for fear of threatening its neutrality.

This neutrality was harshly tested by two world wars. The first spared Switzerland but left it prey to a deep economic stagnation. As for the second, for 50 years the official line was that Switzerland had resisted entering the war thanks to its army and the will of its leaders and its people. In recent years, however, American investigators have uncovered the existence of Jewish funds confiscated by the Nazis during the war and deposited in Swiss bank accounts. In the aftershock of this discovery, the Swiss people are painfully having to rewrite their history.

It seems evident today that this small country, despite the real and courageous mobilisation of its army and people, could never have stood apart from the atrocities of the war without making certain compromises with the Nazi regime. Encircled for four years by Axis powers, Switzerland was forced to maintain most of its commercial relations with those countries. The leaders of that time had to make a choice between the preservation of the country and a morally irreproachable neutrality. Today, a more realistic and human vision is emerging: weaknesses and strengths coexisted here, as they did everywhere.

The concept of neutrality, along with that of direct democracy, remains at the heart of Switzerland's concerns, not only for historical reasons, but also for economic and political ones. However, in a change of heart after 50 years, the Swiss voted to join the UN in 2002. Yet isolation remains a feature of Swiss politics – only a year before voting yes to the UN, the Swiss rejected the opportunity to join the EU. Unconvinced of the benefits of joining such a Union, for the moment the Swiss prefer to simply observe the growing coalition, while remaining at the heart of the continent.

Statue of Justice atop the Fountain of Justice in Bern

Historical Landmarks

58BC Helvetians attempt to invade Gaul and are pushed back by Julius Caesar; Romans begin to colonise Swiss territory.

AD260 First invasion of the Alemanni.

6th century Arrival of the Franks.

9th century Swiss territories incorporated into the Holy Roman Empire.

11th–13th century Habsburg family acquires territory in the area.

13th century Commercial importance of the 'Alpine corridor' grows.

1291 Pact between Uri, Schwyz and Unterwalden: the first Confederation.

1315 The Waldstätten crush Austrian troops at Morgarten; beginning of the military power of the Confederates.

1515 Defeat at the Battle of Marignano; the end of Swiss military power.

1525 The beginning of the Reformation in Switzerland.

1536 The Confederation spreads to the French-speaking regions.

1685 Revocation of the Edict of Nantes; many Huguenots go into exile.

1798 France imposes a Republican structure on Switzerland.

1803 Return to federalism; six new cantons join the Confederation.

1815 Congress of Vienna consecrates Swiss independence and neutrality.

1847 The war of Sonderbund.

1848 The modern Confederation; central government established in Bern.

1863 Creation of the Red Cross in Geneva.

1914–18 Switzerland maintains its neutrality.

1937 Labour unions renounce the right to strike.

1939–45 Switzerland stays out of World War II.

1971 Swiss women win the right to vote in federal elections.

1979 French-speaking part of Jura secedes: birth of a 23rd canton.

1992 Referendum votes against joining European Economic Community, but for participation in the IMF and the World Bank.

2001 In a referendum, the Swiss vote to stay out of the European Union.

2002 Switzerland joins the United Nations.

2005 Swiss voters approve the Schengen Agreement, opening up the borders to citizens from other European countries.

2007 The right-wing Swiss People's Party (SVP) win the general election.

WHERE TO GO

Nothing could be easier than getting around Switzerland *(see page 168)*. The motorway network is excellent, trains and buses service the most remote villages, and urban transport is extremely efficient.

This chapter contains some suggestions for trips within the country. They contain most of the important sites and should help you to plan your itinerary efficiently. The country has been divided into 12 regions that more or less correspond to those given by the Swiss tourist office.

Exploring more than one region a day is not impossible, but we don't recommend that you visit Switzerland at a racing pace. You will probably make your best discoveries off the beaten track. And don't forget that places that look close together on the map may not be so in reality. You may be overlooking the mountain ranges and hairpin turns that lie between one spot and the next.

ZURICH AND VICINITY

Greater Zurich (with one million inhabitants), at the extreme north of the lake of the same name, is Switzerland's largest urban centre. The city has been a major financial capital since its stock exchange was founded in 1877 but, despite its economic importance, the atmosphere of this town remains warm and human – earning it the nickname, the 'Big Small Town'.

The known history of **Zurich** *(Zürich)* goes back to the Neolithic period, when men built villages on piles along the banks of Lake Zurich *(Zürichsee)*. Two thousand years ago, the Romans established a tax office, Turicum, for goods trafficked

The Matterhorn – one of the world's most recognisable peaks

Reflections on Bahnhofstrasse, Zurich's elegant shopping street

along the Limmat River. This spot, today known as the Lindenhof, constitutes the geographic centre of the city. It took another thousand years for Zurich to be recognised as a city, and then to gain fame as a prosperous industrial centre specialising in silk, wool and linen weaving. In 1351, when Zurich joined the Confederation, its noblemen and merchants agreed to share their power with representatives from the tradesmen's guilds, whose guildhalls are still among the treasured monuments of the old town.

In the 16th century, Ulrich Zwingli brought the Reformation to Zurich, adding intellectual renown to the growing commercial and political importance of the city. Through the centuries, the city has distinguished itself as a centre of liberal ideas, attracting a number of great men, such as Goethe, Wagner, Thomas Mann, Einstein, James Joyce, Lenin and Trotsky (these last two spent innumerable hours together at Zurich's Café de l'Odéon). It was from Zurich that Lenin and his Bolshevik colleagues departed, in 1917, aboard the famous 'sealed train' that crossed Germany to reach chaotic St Petersburg.

It was also in Zurich, at the Cabaret Voltaire on the Spiegelgasse, that the Dadaist art movement was born during World War I. Nowadays, the city has over 50 galleries exhibiting all kinds of artwork. The University of Zurich, Switzerland's largest, and the famous Federal Polytechnic (now the Swiss Federal Institute of Technology), considered one of the world's best engineering schools, set the intellectual tone for the city.

Discovering Zurich

The Limmat river symbolises the division between the modern, commercial city and the old town with its characterful narrow streets. The most elegant shopping street in Switzerland and one of the most prestigious in the world, the **Bahnhofstrasse** (1.5km/1 mile), connects the railway station to the lakefront. Jewellery, watches, haute couture, antiques and *objets d'art*: all the most luxurious items can be found here. Shaded by linden trees, the street is reserved for pedestrians, making it ideal for window-shopping. Not far from the station, one stunning building will catch your eye: it's the observatory tower, the **Urania** (open Tues–Sat 9–11pm; <http://urania.astronomie.ch>), with the highest bar in the city. The observatory has a telescope with a magnification factor of 600.

The venerable **Fraumünster** (open May–Sept 9am–6pm, Mar–Apr and Oct 10am–5pm, Nov–Feb 10am–4pm; free) dominates the west bank of the Limmat and overlooks the Münsterhof. There has been a church on this spot since a convent was founded here in 853. The current edifice dates from the 13th century and has a lovely Romanesque choir with **stained-glass windows** designed by Marc Chagall.

Nearby stands the most beautiful baroque building in Zurich, the **Zunfthaus zur Meisen** (open Tues–Sun 10.30am–5pm; admission fee), built in 1757 to serve as

Chagall's glass

In 1967, at the age of 80, Marc Chagall began designing the famed stained-glass windows of the Fraumünster. Three years later they became one of Zurich's most visited attractions, and they still are today.

the wine merchants' guildhall. Today it houses a collection of ceramics from the Swiss National Museum. Also on the Münsterhof, the **Zunfthaus zur Waag** is older still, dating from 1637. Once home to the linen weavers' and hatmakers' guilds, it is now a restaurant, as are many old guild houses.

Charming little streets lined with boutiques and antiques shops lead you to the **Sankt Peterskirche** (Saint Peter's Church; open Mon–Fri 8am–6pm, Sat 9am–4pm, Sun noon–5pm; free), the oldest church in Zurich. Its 13th-century bell-tower houses one of the largest clocks in Europe, more than 9m (30ft) in diameter. The baroque-style nave is decorated with pillars of pinkish-orange marble, delicate stucco and crystal chandeliers dating from the 18th century.

If you are willing to take on the steep stairs leading to the **Lindenhof**, you can enjoy a beautiful view over the Limmat, with its flat-roofed pleasure boats and the busy Limmatquai.

Zunfthaus zur Zimmerleuten, the house of the carpenters' guild

This square's fountain was built in honour of the women of Zurich, who saved the city when it was besieged by the Habsburgs in 1292. Parading in full battle dress, they duped the enemy into believing that the city was too well defended to be conquered.

On the other side of the river, facing the Fraumünster, stands the cathedral, **Grossmünster** (open Apr–Oct Mon–Sat 9am–6pm, Sun 12.30–5pm, Nov–Mar Mon–Sat 10am–5pm, Sun 1–5pm; free), built between 1100 and

Stained glass by Giacometti in the Grossmünster

1250 on the site of a 9th-century church. The Grossmünster is the uncontested 'mother church' of the Reformation in German-speaking Switzerland; Zwingli preached here from 1519 until his death in 1531. The stained-glass windows, designed by Augusto Giacometti, are a 20th-century addition. The twin towers, built in the 15th century and topped with domes from the 18th, are the city's most distinctive landmark. Windows by the same Giacometti also adorn the **Wasserkirche**, oddly situated astride the Limmat.

On the east bank of the river stand the ancient guild houses, each more splendid than the last: the **Zunfthaus zum Rüden**, one-time gathering-place of the nobility; the **Zunfthaus zur Zimmerleuten**, the house of the carpenters' guild, built in 1708 and decorated with oriel windows; and the **Zunfthaus zur Saffran**, headquarters of the haberdashers' guild. Opposite the latter is the **Rathaus** (Town Hall), dating from 1698. Zurich's municipal and cantonal parliaments still meet here.

After visiting the old town, take a stroll along the banks of the lake. The east side offers one surprising spot – the **Chinese Garden** (open Mar–Oct Mon–Sun 11am–7pm; admission fee), a gift to Zurich from its twin city of Kunming. Birds, flowers, fish, streams and bridges – everything here has a flavour of the East. Along the lakefront, the **Zürichhorn** park has two wonderful attractions. The **Heidi Weber house** (open Jun–Sept Sat–Sun 2–5pm; admission fee), Le Corbusier's last work, is a refined mix of forms and colours. A little further along, you'll find *Heureka* – a fantasmagoric extraterrestrial bird, created by sculptor Jean Tinguely.

Zurich's Museums

The **Kunsthaus** (Fine Arts Museum; open Tues, Sat–Sun 10am–6pm, Wed–Fri 10am–8pm; admission fee; <www.kunsthaus.ch>) contains collections of European painting from the Middle Ages to the 20th century, with Swiss artists particularly well represented. On view are works by Johann Heinrich Füssli (1742–1825), Arnold Böcklin and Ferdinand Hodler, both major figures of the 19th century, as well as the sculptor Alberto Giacometti. In addition to masterpieces by Monet, Cézanne, Van Gogh and Picasso, the museum possesses the largest collection outside Scandinavia of works by the Norwegian artist Edvard Munch.

One entire gallery is devoted to Marc Chagall, while another has Dadaist works by Hans Arp, Francis Picabia and Max Ernst. The museum owns collections from several important foundations, including the Alberto Giacometti Foundation, the Dada collection (with, most notably, the photographs of Man Ray) and the Swiss Photography Foundation.

The **Schweizerisches Landesmuseum** (Swiss National Museum; open Tues–Sun 10am–5pm; admission fee; <www.musee-suisse.com>), located in a curious Victorian-style edifice behind the Hauptbahnhof, celebrates the culture, art and history of Switzerland. Its halls are bursting with medieval sculpture and painting, and many rooms feature windows and frescoes that have been removed from ancient churches and houses and re-installed here. Upstairs, a huge room displays weapons, armour, uniforms and other military memorabilia. The museum also has reconstructed rooms from Swiss homes of several centuries ago.

Don't neglect the **Rietberg Museum** and Park Villa Rieter (open Tues–Sun 10am–5pm, Wed until 8pm Apr–Sept; admission fee; <www.rietberg.ch>), tucked away in a luxurious exotic park. The museum contains traditional Chinese scroll paintings, Armenian carpets, Indian statues, Peruvian pottery, African masks and the like, all of which were assembled by the Baron von der Heydt.

Landesmuseum

The **Kunsthalle** (Museum of Contemporary Art; open Tues–Fri noon–6pm, Thur until 8pm, Sat–Sun 11am–5pm; admission fee; <www.kunsthallezurich.ch>) shows international works in a 1,300 sq m (4,265 sq ft) exhibition space.

Excursions

For an amazing panoramic view of Zurich, its lake and the Alps, take the train up to **Uetliberg** (871m/2,860ft) from the central train station or the Selnau station. The trip takes 25 minutes, and there is a train every half-hour.

View from Feusisberg over Lake Zurich in winter

To explore Zurich by the Limmat river, take one of the glass-topped boats that depart from the Landesmuseum every half-hour (from April to October) for a 50-minute tour. Cruises are also available to the **Zürichsee** (several options are available from Burkliplatz pier, ranging from 1½ to 7 hours; lunch is provided on some trips) during which you can admire the lakeside villages surrounded by orchards, vineyards and appealing inns. The villages, especially those on the right bank (nicknamed the 'Gold Coast'), make up Zurich's wealthier suburbs.

Winterthur

Fifteen minutes from Zurich by road or train, **Winterthur** – known by the Swiss as Winti – is largely a commercial town, but it also has a graceful historic centre with plenty of green spaces, artistic monuments and buildings constructed between the 16th and 18th centuries. It is said that Winterthur is the town with the largest number of works of art per capita in the world. It owes this pre-eminence to the generosity of wealthy art patrons such as Oskar Reinhart, who left his collection to the town upon his death in 1965.

Half of the collection is displayed in a massive 19th-century building located in the middle of town. The **Oskar Reinhart Foundation** (open Tues 10am–8pm, Wed–Sun 10am–5pm; admission fee) brings together some 500 choice works by Swiss, German and Austrian artists of the 18th, 19th and 20th centuries. Note in particular the rooms devoted to the work of the German landscape painter Caspar David Friedrich. And don't miss the portraits, landscapes and narrative paintings of Ferdinand Hodler. In the northern part of town, **Am Römerholz** (open Tues–Sun 10am–5pm, Wed until 8pm; admission fee; <www.roemerholz.ch>), the villa where Reinhart himself lived, is home to the remainder of the collection; highlights include works by Cranach the Elder, Brueghel, Cézanne and Van Gogh.

Not far from the Reinhart Foundation, the **Kunstmuseum** (Fine Arts Museum; open Tues 10am–8pm, Wed–Sun 10am–5pm; admission fee) shows interesting work by both Swiss artists (Füssli, Hodler, Vallotton) and French masters (Renoir, Rodin, Bonnard), as well as a superb Quentin Metsys, *Christ Giving His Blessing*.

At Oberwinterthur, northeast of the town, industry is the order of the day: **Technorama** (open Tues–Sun 10am–5pm; admission fee; <www.technorama.ch>) showcases various aspects of technology, from household arts to industrial design, from the earliest motors to the latest computers.

Not to be missed is the **Fotomuseum Winterthur** (open Tues–Sun 11am–6pm, Wed until 8pm; admission fee; <www.fotomuseum.ch>), installed in an abandoned fabric factory, the first and only museum in German-speaking Switzerland devoted entirely to photography. It hosts five important touring exhibitions each year, and its reputation is still growing.

NORTHEAST SWITZERLAND

Commercial and industrial, but also with its fare share of natural beauty, this is one of the least celebrated areas of the country, often sidelined by tourists anxious to get to the household names further south. The region extends from Lake Constance *(Bodensee)* on the border with Germany to the peaks of the canton of Glarus to the south, encompassing the green and peaceful hills of the Appenzell in between.

Schaffhausen

Industrial centre and communications nexus along the Rhine, **Schaffhausen** is the capital of Switzerland's northernmost canton, jutting into German territory like a lost puzzle piece. The heart of the old town, today a pedestrian zone, includes some of the most beautiful façades of the Swiss past.

Houses from the 16th, 17th and 18th centuries are adorned with statues, reliefs, sumptuous allegorical frescoes and richly sculpted oriel windows typical of this region. In 1570, Tobias Stimmer decorated the façade of the **Haus zum Ritter**, a house in the Vordergasse, with frescoes inspired by Roman myth and history. Note also, among the houses on the **Fronwagplatz**, the imposing **Grosses Haus**, which blends Gothic, baroque and rococo styles. The **Haus zum Goldenen Ochsen**, in the Vorstadt, is a Renaissance house noted for its sculpted decorations representing the five senses.

Chutes du Rhin

Heading down river from Schaffhausen, you arrive at the Chutes du Rhin (Rheinfall), the largest waterfall in Europe. Shuttles bring you here from town. With a volume of up to 1,080 cu m (240,000 gallons) every second, these falls are as impressive as they are noisy. Take a boat to the promontory, in the middle of the river, where you can feel the current's full force.

To the south, the 12th-century monastery of **Allerheiligen** (All Saints; open Tues–Sun 11am–5pm; admission fee) now houses a museum rich in illuminated manuscripts and incunabula.

The **Munot** (open daily May–Sept 8am–8pm, Oct–Apr 9am–5pm; free), a vast circular fortress from the 16th century, dominates the town. From its dungeon, a spiral staircase allows access to the roof, from where there is a view of the town, the Rhine flowing through it and the surrounding vineyards.

Stein am Rhein, situated on the right bank of the river (19km/12 miles east of

Chutes du Rhin (Rheinfall)

Schaffhausen), is a wonderful little town. Around the **market square** (Marktplatz) and in the small streets surrounding it, you can find frescoed, half-timbered houses with stepped gables and oriel windows. Some of these buildings date from the 16th century. Often, their decorations illustrate their names: House of the White Eagle, Inn of the Sun, House of the Red Ox and so on.

The **Kloster Sankt Georgen** (Convent of St George; open Apr–Oct Tues–Sun 10am–5pm; admission fee), facing the town hall, was founded by Benedictines in the 11th century. Today, it is a museum of art and history. You can also visit the monks' cells, which have sculpted ceilings decorated with monochromatic frescoes.

The baroque Stiftsbibliothek, St-Gallen's Abbey Library

St-Gallen

Capital of lace and textiles, **St-Gallen** *(Sankt Gallen)* is located 85km (53 miles) from Zurich, between Lake Constance and the lower Alps of northeastern Switzerland. This dynamic city is an excellent example of the successful cohabitation of past and present, where medieval façades rub shoulders with modern buildings and trendy bars.

St-Gallen owes its name and existence to an Irish monk, Gallus, who settled here at the beginning of the 7th century. A hundred years later, a monastery was founded here in his memory, and a city soon sprang up around the abbey, with houses and artisans' workshops, a school and library. Here, monks practised the arts of manuscript illumination, poetry, and music, making St-Gallen a centre for Germanic culture.

In the old town, various abbatial buildings surround the **cathedral** *(Kathedrale)*, one of the last great baroque churches to be built in Europe (in the 1760s). Given the sobriety of the exterior, the white stucco and gold detailing of the interior are all the more striking.

The work these monks devoted themselves to 1,000 years ago is conserved at the **Stiftsbibliothek** (Abbey Library; open Mon–Sat 10am–5pm, Sun 10am–4pm; admission fee; <www.stiftsbibliothek.ch>), which occupies the west wing of the monastery buildings. Before entering, you will notice above the door the Greek inscription *psyche iatreion*, 'apothecary of the soul'. In this room, itself a treasure of baroque art, the shelves, which reach as high as the frescoed ceiling, contain some 100,000 volumes. The collection of manuscripts and incunabula – one of the richest in the world – comprises about 3,600 works. Manuscripts dating from the 9th to the 16th century are displayed in glass cases, the most precious being Irish, Carolingian and Ottonian illuminated manuscripts. To find your way around, look up at the cherubs over your head: they indicate the subjects of books in various parts of the room. For example, the cherub with his eye glued to a telescope is looking at the shelves devoted to astronomy.

Appenzell

The geographic location and the customs of this region make it one of Switzerland's most traditional, a place that looks entirely like a picture-perfect Swiss postcard. The canton of Appenzell is divided into two parts: Inner Rhoden and Ausser Rhoden.

The cantonal seat of Inner Rhoden is **Appenzell**, a small town noted for its

Picture-postcard Appenzell

Appenzell cows

One of the best times to visit Appenzell is in late June and early July, when the farmers drive the cows up into the high Alpine pastures (*Alpaufzug*), or when they bring them back down again in late August or September. These are highly festive events: men in traditional red waistcoats and yellow breeches, wearing hats trimmed with edelweiss flowers, lead their herds of cows or goats, which are themselves decked out with cowbells and festive flowers.

brightly painted wooden houses. In the souvenir stores, you can find handmade Appenzell embroideries, wooden buckets, cowbells, cheeses and naïve paintings by local farmer-artists. If you want to know more about regional art and history, it is worth heading to the **Appenzell Museum** (open daily Apr–Oct 10am–noon, 2–5pm, Nov–Mar Tues–Sun 2–5pm; admission fee), located on the Hauptgasse.

Larger than Appenzell, **Herisau** is the cantonal seat of Ausser Rhoden; here you will also find a museum devoted to the history and craftsmanship of the region.

If the pastoral charm of this corner of paradise moves you, don't miss the picturesque villages of **Urnäsch**, **Gais** (known for its central square lined with 18th-century gabled houses) or **Trogen** with its own *Landsgemeinde* (open-air debate and vote), held every other year. In **Stein** you can also learn the secrets of Appenzell cheesemaking at the **Appenzeller Schaukäserei** (open Apr–Oct daily 9am–7pm, Nov–Mar Mon–Fri 9am–5pm, Sat–Sun 9am–6pm; free).

The mountain of **Säntis** (2,503m/8,212ft) looms over this region. The roads leading to the mountain end at Schwägalp; from here, a cable car, in service year round, will take you to the top. Before your eyes spreads a panorama which extends from the Bernina range in the Grisons Alps, to Lake Constance.

NORTHWEST SWITZERLAND

Northwest Switzerland is the region encompassing the four German-speaking cantons, which include Basel-Stadt, Basel-Land, Solothurn and Aargau.

Basel

The principal metropolis in northwest Switzerland, **Basel** *(Bâle)* is the third-largest city in the country (pop. 165,000). It is also a major Rhine port, linking Switzerland with the sea; it is from here that Swiss exports begin their journey down the Rhine to Rotterdam. An international commercial crossroads, this great industrial centre is nonetheless quite charming thanks to parks, notable architecture and, as always, the river itself. Basel acquired its reputation as a great cultural centre as long ago as the 7th century. In

Basel's Mittlere Rheinbrücke (Middle Bridge) and cathedral

1033, the German emperor, Konrad II, captured the town from the Burgundians, and Basel remained German until 1501, when it became the 11th member of the Swiss Confederation. In 1521, when the scholar Erasmus chose to teach here, the city (whose university, founded in 1460, is the country's oldest) became one of the great humanist centres north of the Alps.

Today, Basel is Zurich's rival for the title of Switzerland's richest city. Three hundred years ago, the bourgeoisie made its living in the silk trade; nowadays, the pharmaceutical and chemical industries are the primary sources of wealth. Each year, the Industrial Fair attracts more than a million visitors, and Basel's stock exchange is fast catching up with Zurich's.

Exploring the City

Our tour begins at the **Mittlere Rheinbrücke** (Middle Bridge), where you can enjoy excellent views of the whole city, crowned by the cathedral and the magnificent medieval buildings that surround it.

Make your way into **Kleinbasel** (Little Basel): from the Oberer Rheinweg you have a splendid view of **Grossbasel**

Fifes and Drums

The Basel Carnival (*Fasnacht*) is famous throughout Europe. It is a colourful three-day festival, with masks, drums and fifes, extraordinary costumes and giant lanterns. On the Monday after Ash Wednesday, at 4am, all the lights of the city go out; after a few impressive minutes of silence, lanterns are lit and, all over the city, the dance groups begin their march to the haunting rhythm of fifes and drums: this is the *Morgestraich*. While processions ebb and flow through the narrow streets, restaurants and cafés fill to the brim, politicians become fair game for satirists, and work and business take second place, or surrender completely.

(Greater Basel), which is older and more aristocratic than its smaller partner. Make a point of seeing the sculpture on the building at Schifflände 1, of the **Lälle-Keenig**, a medieval king sticking out his tongue. This is Grossbasel's way of showing its contempt for its little brother. But Little Basel gets to have its say on the Day of the Gryphon *(Vogel-Gryff)*, when the Wild Man *(Wilde Mann)*, riding by on a raft, climbs the bridge and does an insolent dance. This burlesque ceremony, every January, sets the tone for the riotous Carnival *(Fasnacht)* period *(see opposite)*.

Drummers at Basel's *Fasnacht*

Climb up the streets of Rheinsprung and Augustinergasse, lined with lovely old houses, to the **Münsterplatz**; this perfectly proportioned square is the site of a **Münster** (former cathedral; open Easter–mid-Oct Mon–Fri 10am–5pm, Sat 10am–4pm, Sun 11.30am–5pm, mid-Oct–Easter Mon–Sat 11am–4pm, Sun 11.30am–4pm; free) that has hardly changed since the 12th century. Note the detailing on the Gothic sculptures of the main portal. The main entrance used to be the Gallusporte, a beautiful Roman doorway. Inside, visitors stop to read the epitaph of Erasmus, who died in Basel in 1536.

The **Stadttheater** (Municipal Theatre) is a big modern building in the Theaterstrasse, facing a terraced square with a whimsical mechanical fountain, the **Fasnachtsbrunnen**,

Basel's 16th-century Rathaus

by Jean Tinguely. The latter is a humorous mixed-media construction, representing nine characters spitting into the water.

The three main commercial streets – Freiestrasse, Falknerstrasse and Gerbergasse – all lead to the **Marktplatz**, where you can mingle with the locals buying fruit, vegetables and flowers. On the square where the market is held stands one of the most striking buildings in all of Basel, the 16th-century **Rathaus** (town hall), adorned with small round turrets, larger towers, arches, Renaissance windows and a glittering gold steeple. The whole edifice, painted a vivid bright red, seems like a gigantic, surreal model – almost like a dolls' house.

In the 14th century, the citizens of Basel surrounded the city with a protective wall, of which just one jewel now remains: the **Spalentor**, the Western gate, topped by a clock tower and flanked by two crenellated guard towers. The sculptures of the Virgin and the prophets were added in the 15th century.

Children and grown-ups alike will appreciate the **Zoologischer Garten** (Zoological Garden, or 'Zolli' for short; open daily May–Aug 8am–6.30pm, Mar, Apr, Sept and Oct 8am–6pm, Nov–Feb 8am–5.30pm; admission fee; <www.zoo basel.ch>), located southwest of town, not far from the railway station. With 4,000 animals of 600 different species on

13 hectares (32 acres) of land, it is the largest zoo in Switzerland. Founded more than a century ago, this serious institute of scientific study was the first zoo in Europe where gorillas, rhinoceros and other species reproduced in captivity.

Basel's Museums

Few museums in the world can rival the riches of the prestigious **Kunstmuseum** (Fine Arts Museum; open Tues, Thur–Sun 10am–5pm, Wed 10am–8pm; admission fee; <www.kunst museumbasel.ch>). The first museum to open to the public in Europe, it is also the most well-attended museum in Basel. The Kunstmuseum contains the most comprehensive collection of Holbeins in the world, as well as works by the likes of Lucas Cranach, Matthias Grünewald, Konrad Witz, Martin Schongauer, Hans Baldung Grien, Albrecht Dürer and Rembrandt. The modern collections include works by Basel native Arnold Böcklin, Claude Monet, Paul Gauguin, Georges Braque, Max Ernst, Salvador Dali, Marc Chagall, Alberto Giacometti and Paul Klee, as well as a good number of Picasso's late works. Among the most popular pieces on display are those of Jean Tinguely, whose whimsical, fanciful creations delight both adults and children.

From the Kunstmuseum, it's just a 10-minute walk to the **Museum für Gegenwartskunst** (Museum of Contemporary Art; open Tues–Sun 11am–5pm; admission fee; <www.kunst museumbasel.ch>), which is located on the banks of the Rhine and housed in a converted paper mill. The main hall, lined with glass, houses

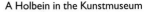
A Holbein in the Kunstmuseum

The Jean Tinguely Museum, filled with mechanical sculptures

Jonathan Borofsky's *Flying Man*, hanging at a third-floor height. The conceptual and minimalist creations of Frank Stella, Donald Judd, Carl André and Joseph Beuys stand in contrast to the extravagant new expressionism of Mimmo Paladino, Enzo Cucchi and Francesco Clemente. The new generation of Swiss artists is also well represented.

In the same contemporary spirit, the **Kunsthalle** (open Tues–Fri 11am–6pm, Thur until 8.30pm, Sat–Sun 11am–5pm; admission fee; <www.kunsthallebasel.ch>) has been presenting new names and trends in changing temporary exhibitions for more than a century.

In the Solitudepark, a pastel-pink sandstone and glass building designed by Mario Botta houses the **Jean Tinguely Museum** (open Tues–Sun 11am–7pm; admission fee; <www. tinguely.ch>). The collection brings together 35 years' worth of this artist's remarkable kinetic sculptures: note, in particular, the *Homage to New York* (1960) and *Lola* (1980).

The **Beyeler Foundation** (open daily 10am–6pm, Wed until 8pm; admission fee; <www.beyeler.com>), located in Riehen, contains a remarkable array of works. Among the artists represented here are Cézanne, Van Gogh, Monet, Picasso, Braque, Miró, Matisse, Mondrian, Kandinsky, Warhol, Rauschenberg and Lichtenstein.

Excursion from Basel

To the east of Basel, **Augst**, the ancient town of Augusta Raurica, is sometimes called the 'Swiss Pompeii'. The 20,000 inhabitants of this flourishing Roman outpost (founded around 44BC) enjoyed a theatre, temple, forum and baths, the ruins of which are still visible. A museum preserves all the artifacts found in digs at this site. In the summer, productions are mounted in the outdoor theatre. (Most sites open daily; admission fee for museum; <www.augustaraurica.ch>.)

Solothurn

This small town is built on the Aare River, at the foot of the Jura range, around 65km (41 miles) south of Basel and 38km (24 miles) north of Bern. **Solothurn**'s past goes back to Roman times, but it is the baroque atmosphere that gives the town its special allure. In the 17th and 18th centuries, Solothurn *(Soleure)* the town, having resisted the Reformation, became the place of residence for ambassadors and envoys from Catholic France, who lived in fine patrician mansions.

The monumental **Sankt Ursenkathedrale** (Cathedral of St-Ursen) is built in a remarkable baroque Italian style. Its treasures include many precious relics, including the Hornbach Missal, an illuminated manuscript from the 10th century.

The **Altes Zeughaus** (Arsenal; open May–Oct Tues–Sun 10am–noon, 2–5pm, Nov–Apr Tues–Fri 2–5pm, Sat–Sun 10am–noon, 2–5pm; admission fee; <www.museum-alteszeughaus.ch>), dating from the 15th century, is close to the main street (Hauptgasse). It contains a fine collection of arms and uniforms from the Middle Ages to the present day.

As you stroll down the Hauptgasse, you will see the **Jesuitenkirche** (Jesuit Church), a baroque building completed near the end of the 17th century. The best place to view the 12th-century **Zeitglockenturm** (clock tower) is from the terrace of a café on the market square. This astronomical clock, meticulously decorated with tiny figures, is over four centuries old.

Solothurn has many small town squares, each one with its own historic fountain. Notice the old houses with their heavy, overhanging roofs and dormer windows of a peculiar local design. Two medieval gateways, the Bieltor and the Baseltor, guard the entrance to the old town.

Beyond the fortifications, in the Werkhofstrasse, is the town's **Kunstmuseum** (Fine Arts Museum; open Tues–Fri

The 17th-century baroque Jesuit Church in Solothurn

11am–5pm, Sat–Sun 10am–5pm; voluntary admission fee), which is worth a visit, if only to see the masterful *Madonna of Solothurn*, by Hans Holbein the Younger.

Baden

Just 22km (14 miles) northeast of Zurich, **Baden** (literally, 'Baths') wears its name well. Two thousand years ago, the Romans were already taking dips in the hot springs of the *Aquae Helveticae* (Swiss waters). Today, visitors taking the waters enjoy luxurious surroundings in local hotels or municipal baths. Rich in mineral salts, these waters are recommended for the treatment of rheumatism, as well as neurological, respiratory and cardiovascular problems.

Begin your visit at one of the highest points in the town: the park facing the casino *(Kursaal)*, or the modern bridge spanning the Limmat river. From here, the view of the old town stretches out before you, down to the water.

Baden's **clock tower** *(Stadtturm)*, constructed in the late Gothic style, dominates the old town. The crenellated wall that climbs the hill connects the clock to a fortress, in ruins since the beginning of the 18th century.

Inside the 15th-century **Rathaus** is an historic room *(Tag-saztungssaal)*, where the representatives of the 13 original cantons met regularly between 1424 and 1712.

If you follow the ancient, winding streets back to the river, past a covered bridge dating from the 19th century, you will reach the **Landvogteischloss** (Bailiff's Castle; open Tues–Fri 1–5pm, Sat–Sun 10am–5pm; admission fee). Inside, a museum displays armaments and other artifacts from the canton of Aarav.

The Sydney and Jenny Brown galleries at the **Langmatt Collection** (Römerstrasse 30; open Apr–Nov Tues–Fri 2–5pm, Sat–Sun 11am–5pm; admission fee; <www.langmatt. ch>) feature a sizeable selection of Impressionist works.

A stroll along Marktgasse, one of Bern's main shopping streets

BERN AND VICINITY

The canton of Bern stretches from the French border in the northwest to the heights of the Alps in the south. Because of the diversity of the terrain, its towns and natural attractions, tourist authorities tend to divide it in two: the federal capital and the northern part of the region as one unit, and Interlaken and the alpine resorts – the Bernese Oberland – as another.

Bern

Bern *(Berne)* has been the capital of the Swiss Confederation since 1848 and with a population of 140,000 is one of Europe's smallest capitals. It is considered one of the best-preserved medieval cities on the continent and is listed by UNESCO as one of the world's cultural treasures. It is also one of the most 'blooming' towns in Europe: in addition to its many public gardens and forests, the façades and historic fountains are covered with flowers. The city, seat of the federal government and of numerous diplomatic offices, as well as various international organisations, remains an enclave of romantic calm.

Bern was founded in 1191 by Duke Berchtold V of Zähringen, who, looking for an impregnable bastion at the western frontier of his lands, decided to perch it on a rocky projection that was formed

The Bern bear

The bear representing the Zähringen family is everywhere: in statue form, on the flag and even alive and well in the Bear Pit *(see page 50)*. Legend has it that when Duke Berchtold V decided to build the city, he swore to name it after the first animal he brought back from the hunt; that animal turned out to be a bear (*Bär*, in German).

by a curve in the Aare river. In 1405, after a fire that destroyed nearly all its wooden houses, Bern was rebuilt in sandstone.

In 1353, after fighting the Habsburgs to defend its independence and freedom, Bern joined the Confederation. The expansion of its holdings to the west brought the French-speaking regions into the Confederation. In 1848, Bern was chosen to be the seat of the federal government.

The Old Town

Begin your exploration of Bern at the railway station: you will discover that the underground shopping galleries here contain the remains of the Christoffelturm (Saint Christopher Tower), part of the old city ramparts.

Take the escalator to street level, to emerge at the start of a lively shopping street, the **Spitalgasse**, where major department stores hide behind elegant old façades. Most of the streets of the old town are edged by covered arcades, making up a promenade 6km (4 miles) long. Under the arcades, you can stroll peaceably in any weather, enjoying the musicians and street artists along the way.

The Zeitglockenturm clock

Bern is full of **fountains**, most of them dating from the 16th century. Their columns generally support allegorical figures painted in bright colours. The first one you will come across is the Pfeiferbrunnen (Bagpiper Fountain), which is probably the work of Hans Gieng, who designed many of these attractive local landmarks.

Further down Spitalgasse lies the **Käfigturm** (17th century) which was once a watchtower, later a prison. Turn left into Waisenhausplatz, where you will see the Waisenhaus (orphanage), a beautiful 18th-century building. The modern fountain nearby, designed by Meret Oppenheim, is a controversial addition. South of the Käfigturm, the Bärenplatz, home to cafés and giant open-air chessboards, is always lively.

Two more fine fountains can be found on **Marktgasse** (return to the Käfigturm and turn right): one is an allegory of *Temperance* – a woman diluting wine with water, in homage to Anna Seiler, founder of the Island Hospital, who donated her house to take in victims of epidemics – while the other, the Schützenbrunnen (Arquebusier Fountain), is decorated with a flag-bearer. Local legend claims that the ogre-topped **Kindlifresserbrunnen**, on the Kornhausplatz (to your left at the end of the Marktgasse), was built to scare children. The **Kornhaus**, once a grain depository, is now a cultural centre hosting exhibitions and other events. This group of buildings also includes the Fine Arts and Industrial Arts libraries. Don't hesitate to take a seat in the Kornhaus Café, a successful combination of ancient walls and modern touches.

The **Zeitglockenturm** (clock tower), the oldest monument in Bern, is so unusual you might want to organise your visit around it, so you can witness this extraordinary display of 16th-century Swiss clockwork. Arrive at least five minutes before the hour and prepare to take in the show: a jester contorts himself to ring two bells above his head, a procession of bears follows, a rooster crows and flaps his wings, Father Time turns over his hourglass, and so on.

Beyond the Zeitglockenturm, on the **Kramgasse**, the Zähringerbrunnen (Zähringen Fountain) is topped by a bear in armour, with a baby bear at his feet. The *Mutz*, as Bern natives have nicknamed him, was built in honour of the city's founder. Albert Einstein and his family lived from 1902 to 1909 at number 49 on the Kramgasse. The apartment where the physicist developed his theory of relativity has been converted into a small museum.

Located further down the Kramgasse, and one street to the left, is the **Rathaus**, a ravishing Gothic construction that rises

$E = mc^2$

In 1905, while working at the Swiss Patent Office in Bern, a young Albert Einstein spent much time thinking about a multitude of theories concerning light, space and time. It was in this year, called the *Annus Mirabilis* (Miracle Year), that Einstein developed the Special Theory of Relativity, or $E=mc^2$. He spent most of his time working on this theory and several others, including his Nobel Prize-winning theory on light quantum, at Kramgasse 49, where he lived with his wife and son for several years. A small museum is located here. It is believed that Einstein thought often about Bern's famous Zeitglockenturm to relate light and time as he developed his famous theory.

up between the Postgasse and the Postgasshalde. Note also the colourful Vennerbrunnen (Flagbearer Fountain), which shows a Bernese standard-bearer in full uniform.

As you continue along the Kramgasse, the Gerechtigkeits-gasse features the **Gerechtigkeitsbrunnen**, a fountain representing the allegory of Justice. At the end of the street, you will be faced with two tempting choices: you can cross the bridge and go straight to the Bear Pit, or take a left on the Nydeggstalden to the oldest part of town. After the Nydeg-gkirche (Nydegg Church), head down to the Läuferplatz to see the **Untertorbrücke**, the oldest bridge in Bern (1461–89). To the left, the Läuferbrunnen (Messenger Fountain) pays homage to a herald from Bern who, reproached by the king of France for not speaking French, had the audacity to reply: 'Well, you can't speak German!'

To get to the **Bear Pit** (*Bärengraben*), turn right after the Untertorbrücke and follow the ramp. Bern without its bears would be like Paris without the Eiffel Tower. Bears have enjoyed pride of place here since the 15th century – with the exception of the period of French occupation, during which time the mascots were confiscated. The crowd is at its most dense on Easter morning, when, if weather permits, the mother bears and their new cubs are brought out for the first time each year.

Cross back over the Nydeggbrücke and walk up the Junkerngasse to the **Münster** (open Easter–Oct Tues–Sat 10am–5pm, Sun 11.30am–5pm, Nov–Easter Tues–Fri 10am–noon, 2–4pm, Sat 10am–noon, 2–5pm, Sun 11.30am–2pm; free), Switzerland's most majestic cathedral built in the late Gothic style. It took more than two centuries to complete. The nave, begun in 1421, was only finished 150 years later, and not until 1893 was the openwork spire, 100m (328ft) high, added. The largest of the bells, weighing more than 10 tonnes, was installed in 1611. *The Last Judgement* (1490–95,

Erhart Küng's *Last Judgement* above the Münster's entrance

on the tympanum over the main entrance), a remarkable work by Erhart Küng, represents a series of 234 damned and chosen souls, recruited from every social class. In the choir, the beautiful 15th-century **stained-glass windows** illustrate, in particular, the three kings and an impressive *danse macabre*; don't miss the magnificent Renaissance **choir stalls**. A staircase leads to the second terrace of the tower, with a splendid view of the city.

From the **Münsterplattform**, an incredible lift takes you to the riverbank, in the old popular neighbourhood of **Matte**. Now renovated, the district is full of boutiques, crafts stands and artists' studios, and makes for a very agreeable walk. Near the Münsterplattform, the **Bundeshaus** (Federal Parliament Building), built in the 19th century, is the seat of Swiss government. The building can be visited any time except during Parliamentary sessions and on holidays. During sessions, the visitors' galleries are open.

Climb the Gurten

For a brief excursion, you can climb the Gurten (858m/2,185ft high), where the view of Bern and the surrounding Alps is just extraordinary. It takes about 25 minutes to get to the summit by tramway (the number 9 line), then on the funicular running out of Wabern, just south of the city centre.

Bern's Museums

The **Kunstmuseum** (Fine Arts Museum; open Wed–Sun 10am–5pm, Tues 10am–9pm; admission fee; <www.kunstmuseumbern.ch>), at Hodlerstrasse 12, displays examples of Bernese painting from the Middle Ages to 19th-century Realism as well as a rich collection of modern art with works by Manet, Cézanne, Monet, Renoir, van Gogh and Hodler. There are also works by Paul Klee, who was born in Bern and died here in 1940. Most of the Klee collection, however, has been moved to the **Zentrum Paul Klee** (open Tues–Sun 10am–5pm, Thur until 9pm; admission fee; <www.zpk.org>), 10 minutes by bus or tram from Bern's old town. This museum, which is devoted solely to Klee's work, has around 4,000 paintings.

The **Kunsthalle** (Art Institute; open Tues 10am–7pm, Wed–Sun 10am–5pm; admission fee), located at Helvetiaplatz 1, is devoted to contemporary art and stages temporary exhibitions of avant-garde works.

Mountain-lovers will rush to the **Schweizerisches Alpines Museum** (Swiss Alpine Museum; open Mon 2–5.30pm, Tues–Sun 10am–5.30pm; admission fee; <www.alpinesmuseum.ch>), at Helvetiaplatz 4, where topographic reliefs of the mountains and other maps are on display alongside antique skiing and climbing equipment.

The **Museum Für Kommunikation** (Museum of Communication, open Tues–Sun 10am–5pm; admission fee; <www.mfk.ch>), at Helvetia Strasse 16, tells the story of the postal service, the telegraph and the telephone, from the earliest centralised phones to the most modern teleprinters. Rare stamps, both Swiss and foreign, are on display in the basement.

The **Bernisches Historisches Museum** (Bern Historical Museum; open Tues–Sun 10am–5pm; admission fee; <www.bhm.ch>), in an extraordinary neo-Gothic building at Helvetiaplatz 5, contains artisanal objects as well as armaments, figures and jewellery. Its most precious possession is the booty seized from the Duke of Burgundy in the battle of Grandson (1476), including battle standards, manuscripts and precious tapestries. An exhibition dedicated to Einstein was recently added.

The collections of the **Naturhistorisches Museum** (Museum of Natural History; open Mon 2–5pm, Tues, Thur and Fri 9am–5pm, Wed 9am–7pm, Sat–Sun 10am–5pm; admission fee; <www.nmbe.ch>), at Bernastrasse 15 figure among the richest in Europe. Zoology, geology, mineralogy and palaeontology are particularly well represented and well displayed.

The flower market on Bern's Bundesplatz (Federal Square)

Biel

Prehistory and modern industry live side by side in **Biel** *(Bienne)*, a town of rivers, streams and canals, situated on the lake of the same name about 32km/20 miles northeast of Bern. Its many watchmaking firms give it its nickname, the 'Swiss watch capital'. The town gets its particular character from the bilingual meeting of two cultures (two-thirds of the population speak Swiss German, one-third speak French). The Biennese juggle the two languages without confusion.

The medieval old town is perfect for a leisurely stroll, particularly beneath the arcades of the **Obergasse**. Here, as in Bern, the 16th-century fountains draw the visitor's gaze with their boldly coloured statues. Notice the Vennerbrunnen (Flagbearer Fountain), on the **Ring**, a central plaza surrounded by an impressive architectural ensemble.

The Biennese take their prehistory to heart. It was a native of Biel, Friedrich Schwab (1803–69), who discovered at La Tène (on Lake Neuchâtel) the vestiges of a second Iron Age culture. The objects he excavated belonged to the ancient civilisation known as La Tène and are now on display in the Biel museum named after Schwab.

From Biel, it takes approximately an hour and a half to walk out to the **Taubenloch gorges** (Taubenlochschlucht). A footpath leads to this site of wild beauty, which is known as the gateway to the Jura mountains. **Evilard**, a little village perched on the hills above Biel, offers a marvellous view of the high peaks in the Bernese Oberland lying beyond Bern.

In about 50 minutes, a boat will take you to **St Peter's Island** *(Sankt Petersinkel)*, on Lake Biel. This nature preserve is an island only in name, since drainage lowered the water level during the 19th century, turning St Peter's into a peninsula connected to the mainland. In the 18th century, St Peter's Island so captivated that 'friend of nature' Jean-Jacques Rousseau that he stayed here from 1765 to

1767. The hotel room where the philosopher lived, full of mementos, still attracts nostalgic visitors.

The Emmental

Everything about Switzerland that is rural, green, peaceful and perfectly clean is encapsulated by **the Emmental**. Even the most urban visitor will soon admit that the natural beauty of this region is impossible to resist.

Just 22km (14 miles) northeast of Bern, **Burgdorf** *(Bert-houd)*, which overlooks the Emmental Valley, is a centre for the textile industry. The restored 12th-century castle has a small museum of local history. From Burgdorf, a pretty road follows the valley of the River Emme to the fair-sized village of **Langnau**, some 30km (19 miles) from Bern. Besides its interesting folk museum, Langnau offers an excellent sweet cheese studded with large holes – the delicious Emmental.

View over the Emmental to the Bernese Alps

BERNESE OBERLAND

The Oberland, lying to the south of
Bern, is a region with much to offer
the tourist: majestic mountains,
impressive glaciers, vast lakes and
cascades, charming villages, and
well-equipped holiday resorts.
Since the beginning of the 19th
century, well before skiing and hiking became popular pursuits, the
English and French elite came here
to relax in luxury hotels and to see,
far off, the peak of the Jungfrau.
Some of them even ventured as far
as the glaciers.

Around Lake Thun

Thun *(Thoune)*, tucked into the
northernmost edge of the lake of
the same name, occupies a remarkable site: the centre of the old
town sits on a long, narrow island on the Aare, just where
the river flows out of the lake. This island, small enough to
cross easily on foot, is linked to dry land by several bridges.
Thun's main commercial street, the **Hauptgasse**, is curiously
built on two levels, so that you walk on top of the flower-
bedecked roofs of the stores that line it, while admiring the
windows of a second level of boutiques.

At the end of the street, between numbers 55 and 57, take
the covered staircase leading to the castle and the baroque
parish church. The **Schloss Thun** is a group of fortifications
crowned with a Romanesque tower topped with a smaller
tower at each corner. The **Historisches Museum** (Historical

Museum; open Apr–Oct daily 10am–5pm, Feb–Mar daily 1–4pm, Nov–Jan Sun 1–4pm; admission fee), founded in 1888, occupies three floors of the dungeon. The main room is the Knights' Room, a majestic chamber hung with 15th-century tapestries, with pikes and halberds on display. On the floor above are Swiss military uniforms and armaments from the ancient crossbow to modern-day weapons. On the floor below, you will find artisanal works and a collection of toys.

Old steamboats cross Lake Thun, offering pleasant mini-cruises. Along the north bank, a road leads from the lake to

Above: close-up of the Eiger, Mönch and Jungfrau

the hills, ending at **Oberhofen**. This town is known for its medieval castle, which was reconstructed and sumptuously decorated during the 17th and the 19th centuries and now houses a section of the Bern Historical Museum.

On the south bank of the lake, the town of **Spiez** also has an imposing castle dating from the 12th and 13th centuries. Don't miss the magnificent panoramic view from the **Niesen** (2,632m/8,635ft), an impressive natural pyramid. To reach the top, take the funicular from Mülenen, about 2km (1 mile) south of Spiez.

Several ski resorts can be conveniently reached from Spiez. If you take the road through the Simmental, you will reach **Gstaad**, a resort that has long been fashionable with the world's rich and famous, who come here to ski and be seen in an atmosphere that's decidely chic and in surroundings of great natural beauty.

A paddle steamer cruises Lake Thun

Interlaken

The famous ski centre of **Interlaken** is located, as its name indicates, between the lakes of Thun and Brienz, and offers a splendid view of the Jungfrau mountain, with its perpetual cloak of snow.

Höheweg (or Höhe), a magnificent boulevard shaded by trees, offers gorgeous views of the surrounding peaks. The north side is occupied by grand Victorian-era

St Beatus Caves

Just outside Interlaken on the east bank of Lake Thun lies the natural wonder of the St Beatus Cave carved into the Niederhorn massif. A kilometre (½mile) of caves can be toured by well-lit paths. There is also a small museum and restaurant on-site (open Apr–mid-Oct daily 10.30am–5pm; admission fee; <www.beatushoehlen.ch>).

hotels, restaurants, boutiques and the famous casino *(Kursaal)*. The sunnier and more open southern part features a beautiful park, the **Höhematte**, with a view that opens on to the Jungfrau. You can travel around Interlaken by horse-and-carriage or on foot, or escape the crowds on a hiking trail. From Wildersheim, 2km (1 mile) away, a cog railway climbs up to the **Schynige Platte**. As well as a superb panorama of the Bernese Alps, this site offers visitors a garden of alpine blooms.

Towards the Peaks

Train enthusiasts and armchair alpinists will find it hard to resist the attraction of a comfortable journey from Interlaken to Jungfraujoch, the highest railway station in Europe (3,454m/11,332ft). In clear weather, the spectacle is one of a kind, and the air is extraordinarily pure.

From Interlaken, you can make part of the journey by car to **Grindelwald** (a lively international ski resort) or **Lauterbrunnen**. From either place, the train will take you to the Jungfrau. The construction of this railway – the **Jungfraubahn** (<www.jungfraubahn.ch>) – was one of the great technological achievements of the end of the 19th century. It climbs in a spiral, through tunnels carved into the rock face of the Eiger.

Whether you come from Grindelwald or Lauterbrunnen, you will reach the Jungfraubahn at the **Kleine Scheidegg** (Little Scheidegg) station, at the foot of the awe-inspiring North Wall of the **Eiger**, first conquered in 1938. The mountain is surrounded by the soaring peaks of the **Wetterhorn**, the **Mönch** and the **Jungfrau** (4,158m/13,642ft).

The train then enters an almost continuous series of tunnels (7km/4½ miles) after the Eigergletscher station, where the Eiger glacier looms into view. It also briefly stops at Eigerwand (the Wall of Eiger) and Eismeer (the Ice Sea), for pas-

Cogs and Cable Cars

You can climb a Swiss mountain the hard way, with crampons, a pick and some rope. But an easier method of accessing the pure air of the peaks is to take advantage of technology – technology that, in Switzerland, is breaking records by leaps and bounds.

Since the end of the 19th century, the cog-wheel railways have made communications possible over the mountains. The Viznau-RigiBahn, finished in 1871 by the Swiss engineer Riggenbach, is the oldest cog train in Europe. The Pilatus (Lucerne), which travels on the world's steepest tracks (48°) has been running since 1889. In Zermatt, one of these trains goes as high as Gornergrat (3,130m/10,270ft). Finally, the highest train in Europe climbs to Jungfraujoch, at an altitude of 3,454m (11,332ft).

Cable cars often pick up the next leg of the climb, easily crossing the most difficult zones. The highest line in Europe links Zermatt to the Matterhorn, at more than 3,800m (12,467ft).

Saas-Fee has an Alpine subway, which goes from the Felskinn cable car stop (3,000m/9,838ft) to Mittelallalin (3,500m/11,483ft). Not surprisingly, the Metro Alpin is the highest subway in the world.

sengers to get out for a glimpse of the marvellous view through the 'picture windows' carved in the rock.

Jungfraubahn and the Eiger

The last station is **Jungfraujoch**, where a restaurant and observation terrace dominate the Aletschgletscher, the longest of the Alpine glaciers at 25km (15 miles). Dress warmly, even in summer, and wear appropriate shoes: if weather permits, you can go for a walk (but stay inside the signposted safe areas) or take a ride in a dogsled. The ice sculptures on view at the 'Ice Palace', as well as a small exhibition on scientific research at high altitudes, are worth a look.

Another excursion to undertake in good weather is a trip to the **Schilthorn** mountain, which offers a fine view of the Alps. From Stechelberg and **Mürren** (a romantic village completely without cars, perched on a veritable 'balcony' facing the Eiger, Mönch and Jungfrau mountains), a cable car (<www.schilthorn.ch>) climbs to a height of 2,970m (9,744ft) to leave you at the Piz Gloria revolving restaurant (made famous by the James Bond movie *On Her Majesty's Secret Service*). It takes 50 minutes for the turning platform to complete one rotation, allowing plenty of time for gazing out over the Bernese Alps, Mont Blanc and the Jura and Vosges mountain ranges.

Don't leave this region without having seen the **Trümmelbach Waterfalls** (3km/2 miles from Stechelberg). A lift takes you to the well-lit galleries, where the impressive cascades burst from underground gorges. Don't forget your raincoat.

Brienz Lake

A small blue marvel with wilder and more dramatic surroundings than those of its brother, Lake Thun, the Brienzersee is linked to the Thun by the Aare River.

The town of **Brienz**, on the easternmost point of the lake, is the Swiss capital of wooden sculpture. The town also has a school of wood sculpture, another for the handcrafting of string instruments and several souvenir stores.

The **Brienzer Rothorn** looms over the region from its height of 2,530m (8,300ft). The hour-long journey up the Rothorn, in an old-fashioned railway carriage pulled by a steam engine, reveals scenes of tranquil, breathtaking beauty (<www.brienz-rothorn-bahn.ch>). Another popular excursion begins with a boat or car ride to the wooded bank of the lake facing Brienz; then, from Giessbach See, a funicular transports travellers to the **Giessbach Falls**, a superb series of waterfalls, which hurtle straight down from a height of 400m (1,312ft). Simply one of the most romantic spots imaginable, Giessbach is home to an old hotel that has been beautifully renovated.

Each village and market town of the Oberland has a church, a town hall and a folklore museum. None, however, is as ambitious as the **Open-Air Museum of Ballenberg** (open mid-Apr–Oct daily 10am–5pm; admission fee; <www.ballenberg.ch>), about 2km (1 mile) northeast of Brienz on the route to Brünig. The 'Ballenberg', whose official name is the *Schweizerisches Freilichtmuseum für ländliche Bau- und Wohnkultur*, groups together village houses, some more than three centuries old, brought here from all over the country. Seeing them together underlines the great variety of styles, materials and methods in Swiss construction: the Oberland chalet, for example, with its low roof and highly wrought façade, is very different from the typical house of central Switzerland, in wood and masonry. The interiors are authentically furnished, and the houses have vegetable plots in their back gardens and farm animals. Here and there, artisans demonstrate their craft according to traditional methods.

Meiringen, a pretty little town 20km (12 miles) from Brienz, on the upper banks of the Aare (Haslital), is popular with excursionists and alpinists. Fires in the 19th century destroyed most of the historic buildings, but some wooden constructions typical of the region were saved.

The hike to the **Trift suspension bridge** (tel: 033 972 5151), just east of Meiringen, is a unique high-mountain experience. The rope bridge, which overlooks Lake Trift and the Trift Glacier, is the longest of its kind in Europe. Reaching it requires a 10 minute cable car ride (starting from Oberhasli; open Jul–Sept) and a challenging, vertiginous 90-minute hike, each way.

The Aare Gorge

While you're in the area, you should try to see the deep **Aare Gorge** *(Aareschlucht)*, a striking natural attraction at the foot of the Susten and Grimsel mountain passes. Assiduous readers of Sir Arthur Conan Doyle won't want to miss the nearby **Reichenbach Falls**, reached by funicular (<www.reichenbachfall.ch>). It is here that Sherlock Holmes and his arch-enemy Moriarty plunged together to their deaths. The famous detective later had to be resuscitated, under pressure from readers hungry for new adventures.

LUCERNE AND CENTRAL SWITZERLAND

Here, you are in the land of William Tell, at both the historical and geographical heart of the country. Travellers have been attracted to this lush region since long before the age of tourism. This area includes the cantons of Lucerne, Zug, Uri, Nidwalden and Obwalden.

Lucerne

Just about all the elements of a perfect tourist town converge in **Lucerne** (*Luzern* in German): a splendid waterfront setting against a backdrop of mountains; historic churches, interesting shops, and plenty of greenery; an annual music festival and paddle-wheel excursion boats.

A thousand years ago, Lucerne was a humble fishing village that happened also to be home to a Benedictine monastery. Under the domination of the powerful Alsatian Abbey of Murbach, it became a merchant city; its importance increased with the opening of the St Gotthard pilgrimage route. Citizens of Lucerne enjoyed relative freedom until 1291, the year the Habsburgs took the city. To release itself from their control, Lucerne turned in 1332 to the young Swiss Confederation. After the victory of the Confederates at the battles of Sempach in 1386, Lucerne, now independent, enjoyed a period of prosperity. A Catholic bastion, it remained resistant to the Reformation.

By the 18th century, Lucerne was the country's biggest town and also the centre of Catholic Switzerland. In 1847, while the Catholic cantons were seceding from the Confederation, Lucerne

Secret capital

Many consider Lucerne to be the secret capital of Switzerland: if Bern is the head, and Zurich the hand, then Lucerne can certainly pride itself on being the heart of the country.

placed itself at the head of the rebellion. After the reconciliation, grand hotels were built along the lake; in 1870, the legendary Caesar Ritz opened the Grand National Hotel. Alexander Dumas defined Lucerne as 'a pearl in the world's most beautiful oyster'.

The Old Town

The very model of the Swiss covered bridge, the **Kapellbrücke** (Chapel Bridge), a symbol of Lucerne, was built at the beginning of the 14th century over the Reuss river. It burned down in 1993 – an emotional shock for Lucerners – and was reopened in 1994. More than 100 paint-

The Wasserturm and the Kapellbrücke on the Reuss

ings dating from the 17th century adorn the triangles formed by its ceiling beams, telling the story of the patron saints of the city and of heroes of Lucerne, as well as depicting episodes from Swiss history. The bridge can only be crossed on foot. Until the 19th century the octagonal stone tower alongside it, the **Wasserturm** (Water Tower), was used as a prison, an archival library and a treasury.

A little further along the left bank of the river, the **Jesuitenkirche** (Jesuit Church), begun at the end of the 17th century, is one of the oldest and most beautiful baroque buildings in Switzerland. Its pink-and-white interior, decorated with stucco and frescoes, dates from 1750, while the towers are from 1893. Follow the Bahnhofstrasse away from the banks of the Reuss to reach the **Franziskanerkirche** (Franciscan Church), built in the 13th century in the Gothic style.

Return to the river and follow its course past the Zeughaus, the old arsenal, to cross the **Spreuerbrücke** (Mill Bridge). This covered wooden bridge from the early 15th century is decorated with superb artworks painted between 1625 and 1632. Their theme, a common one in the Middle Ages, is the dance of death.

On the right bank, you enter the most striking part of the city: the **Weinmarkt** (Winemarket Square), the heart of medieval Lucerne. Most of the buildings that encircle it – old guild houses, boutiques and patrician homes – have preserved their elaborately painted façades. Particularly worth a look is the Weinmarktapotheke (Winemarket Pharmacy), built in 1530. Nearby, the **Hirschenplatz** (Deer Square), also surrounded by old houses, used to host the city's hog market.

The houses of the nobility around the **Rathaus** (town hall) are joined by several floors of arcades. One of these houses, the beautiful **Haus Am Rhyn** (open daily Apr–Oct 10am–6pm, Nov–Mar 11am–5pm; admission fee), at Furrengasse 21, is home to a fascinating collection of Picasso's late works. This museum also owns 200 photos of the painter by the photographer David Douglas Duncan. Not far away, the **Rosengart Collection** (open daily Apr–Oct 10am–6pm, Nov–Mar 11am–5pm; <www.rosengart.ch>), at Pilatusstrasse 10, has more works by Picasso, as well as several works of Klee, Monet, Renoir and Cézanne among others.

Turning from the Reuss, walk up to the **Museggmauer**, part of the longest (at 870m/2,854ft) and best-preserved fortifications in Europe. From Easter to October, a section of these 600-year-old ramparts and three of its towers are open to the public. On the **Zyt Tower**, the oldest clock in town (dating from 1535) chimes one minute before every hour.

A short walk takes you past the Museumplatz and the Löwenplatz to **Löwendenkmal** (the Lion monument). What Mark Twain called 'the most lugubrious and moving block of stone on earth' is dedicated to the memory of 800 Swiss mercenaries who died during the French Revolution, in particular in the Tuileries on 10 August 1792, while defending King Louis XVI and his family. This lion, mortally wounded with a blow of the lance, was carved in stone in 1821, after a drawing by the Danish sculptor Bertel Thorvaldsen.

Alongside the lion, you can see the 'giants' tureens' in the **Gletschergarten** (Glacier Garden; open daily Apr–Oct 9am–6pm, Nov–Mar 10am–5pm; admission fee; <www.gletschergarten.ch>). These are deep potholes created 20,000 years ago by the glacier that covered this region. To better understand this geological phenomenon, go to the park museum, where fossils and minerals are on display.

The Löwendenkmal commemorates fallen Swiss mercenaries

Also nearby, the **Bourbaki Panorama** (open Tues–Sun 9am–6pm, Mon 1–6pm; admission fee; <www.bourbaki panorama.ch>), a gigantic round painting illustrating the turning back of French troops commanded by General Bourbaki after their defeat at the hands of the Prussians (January 1871), stands 10m (33ft) tall and 114m (375ft) wide.

The **Verkehrshaus der Schweiz** (Swiss Transport Museum; open daily Apr–Oct 10am–6pm, Nov–Mar 10am–5pm; admission fee; <www.verkehrshaus.ch>), which is always being embellished and updated to keep up with technological progress, is the largest and most complete of its kind in Europe. The aeronautical section has dozens of early aeroplanes, as well as a reconstruction of the Zurich airport control tower, space capsules from the first American space flights and even a moon rock. In the huge section devoted to railway transport, you can find more than 60 real locomotives and a very faithful reproduction of a section of the Saint-Gotthard rail line. Swissorama, projected on to a circular screen, shows a 20-minute film on Switzerland, its culture, traditions and economy. The history of the automobile also has its place here, as do tourism, the postal and telecommunications industries and navigation by river, lake and sea – for, landlocked as it may be, Switzerland is nonetheless a nautical nation. Finally, the museum has a planetarium and a giant-screen IMAX cinema.

Lucerne Festival

Part of the world-famous Lucerne Music Festival takes place in the grounds of the Richard Wagner Museum every August and September. Visit <www.lucernefestival.ch> for more information.

The **Richard Wagner Museum** (open mid-Mar–Nov Tues–Sun 10am–noon, 2–5pm; admission fee; <www.richard-wagner-museum.ch>) occupies Haus Tribschen, the spacious home where the composer lived from 1866 to 1872. It was in this house

Haus Tribschen, home of the Richard Wagner Museum

that he married Cosima, Franz Lizst's daughter. The villa, built on a promontory and commanding a wonderful view, was so dear to Wagner that he declared, 'Nothing will make me leave this place.' (Later, of course, he left it for Bayreuth.) The first floor has a selection of original scores, letters and photographs, along with Wagner's grand piano. Upstairs is the city's collection of antique and exotic instruments.

Lake Lucerne

The most delightful way to visit central Switzerland is to take a steamboat in summer – a motorboat in winter – and to drift down the **Vierwaldstättersee** (Lake Lucerne).

The softly sloping banks of the Swiss plateau, with Mount Pilatus (2,129m/6,985ft; *see page 71*) in the background, give way little by little to the foothills of the lower Alps and their pastures, while the higher peaks tower majestically over the south end of the lake.

Statue of William Tell in Altdorf

The bay of **Küssnacht** is best known for its flowering many orchards and farms with pointed roofs. **Weggis**, **Witznau** and **Beckenried** are pretty villages that invite you to wander or sit down for a meal. Across from Weggis, above the lake, **Bürgenstock**, once one of Europe's most famous ski resorts, still attracts a fashionable clientele. A fascinating one-hour walk brings you to the foot of the impressive Hammetschwand elevator, which gives access to a fabulous view.

The 28m (92ft) rock that rises from the water on the other side of the lake from **Brunnen** is called the Schillerstein. This 'pebble' is dedicated to the great German dramatist, Friedrich Schiller, who immortalised William Tell *(see page 14)* in a famous play. Oddly enough, Schiller never set foot in Switzerland.

A bit further along, the meadow of **Rütli** is the symbol of Swiss national unity: the birthplace of the Confederation, founded here in 1291 *(see page 14)*, it is also the place chosen by General Henri Guisan, in 1940, to gather his top officers to organise a national defence strategy.

Lake Uri with its steep, fjord-like banks, is the wildest branch of the Vierwaldstättersee. While this entire region is particularly well suited to hiking, the 'Swiss road' along the banks of Lake Uri is nothing less than a historical adventure for those who love to walk. Most places here are also accessible by other means (train, boat or bus). The **Tellskapelle**

(Chapel of Tell), on the east bank, is built on the very spot where William Tell is said to have leapt from the boat taking him to prison, thus escaping his jailers.

Flüelen, at the far end of the lake, was once the unloading dock for boats carrying merchandise destined for trade in Italy. The bundles were then loaded on to mules for the journey through the Gotthard pass. **Altdorf**, the county seat of the canton of Uri, owes its fame to William Tell, who shot the apple off his son's head here; at the Tellspielhaus, Schiller's play continually re-enacts the same victory.

Three Mountains

Mount Pilatus. Considered the emblem of Lucerne, it was scaled for the first time in the 16th century. This was a courageous undertaking, not only because it required good mountaineering skills, but because the villagers, believing the

Vierwaldstättersee (Lake Lucerne) viewed from Mount Pilatus

mountain to be haunted by the demonic spirit of Pontius Pilate (hence the name), forbade anyone access to it with threat of imprisonment.

Generally, visitors take the boat or the train to Alpnachstad, then the cog-wheel railway (the steepest route in the world, with a 48° grade; it runs only in summer), which leaves you with a five-minute walk to the top (2,132m/6,995ft), where the view is extensive. As an alternative route down, take the cable car from Kriens (<www.pilatus.ch>).

Mount Rigi. In good weather, there is a superb view from Rigi-Kuhn (1,800m/5,906ft) of the highest peaks of the Alps from Bern to Valais. This 'island in the sun' is accessible by cog train (from Vitznau or Goldau) or cable car (from Weggis). For imetables and fares, see <www.rigi.ch>.

The world's first revolving cable car, on Mount Titlis

Mount Titlis. Nearly twice as high as Rigi, it reaches 3,240m (10,630ft). First, go to **Engelberg**, a sunny ski resort whose Benedictine monastery was founded in the 17th century. Be sure to admire the abbey's baroque church; the organ here is the largest in the country. From the station, take the funicular, then the spectacular revolving cable car (<www. titlis.ch>), to arrive at Klein (Little) Titlis, where the snow never melts; here, you can explore an ice cave and marvel at the peaks of Oberland and the Valais Alps. It takes another hour on foot to cover the last 220m (720ft) of uneven terrain to the very top of Mount Titlis.

East of Lucerne

Whether they like it or not, statistics reveal that the citizens of Zug are the richest inhabitants of Switzerland. In international economy and finance circles, Zug is known as a fiscal paradise, which explains the presence

Façade in Schwyz

here of so many business firms and sumptuous villas.

Small, cosmopolitan and opulent, the town of **Zug** *(Zoug)* owes its charm to its ancient and perfectly preserved stone walls. Modern buildings blend with historic ones in a harmonious and original way. The Fischmarkt (the fish market), the Untergasse and the Obergasse all evoke the Middle Ages. At the corner of the Fischmarkt and the Untergasse, the **Rathaus** (town hall) is remarkable for its magnificent Council Room. Among the vestiges of medieval fortifications, notice in particular the **Zytturm** (clock tower) on the Kolinplatz (ask for the key at the police station next door). Just steps away, the 15th- and 16th-century **Sankt-Oswalds-Kirche** (Saint Oswald's Church) deserves to be seen for the delicate sculptures above its main door. Be sure to continue your visit just behind this church to the exquisite **Burg**, which houses an historical museum.

For a town that gave its name to the whole country, **Schwyz** is rather placid and much smaller than you might

imagine. The **Bundesbriefmuseum** (open Tues–Fri 9–
11.30am, 1.30–5pm, Sat–Sun 9am–5pm, Nov–Apr Sat–Sun
1.30–5pm; admission fee) contains precious documents from
the earliest days of the Confederation: the Pact of 1291, ini-
tialled by the representatives of the 13 original cantons *(see
page 16)*, and a series of charters, each marking a stage in
the fascinating construction of the country.

Einsiedeln, one hour from Lucerne or Zurich, is an important pilgrimage site. Gigantic and imposing, its **Benedictine
abbey** attracts many tourists. The history of Einsiedeln began
more than 1,100 years ago when a monk, Meinrad, was
murdered in his hermitage in the middle of the forest. A century later, he had become the object of cult worship, and
some monks founded a monastery in his memory on the
same site. The church and its surrounding 11th-century
baroque buildings are considered the crowning achievement
of their architect, Caspar Moosbrugger, a converted monk
who lived in Einsiedeln for more than 40 years. At the centre
of the complex is the abbey church, flanked by two towers.
The church suffered bomb damage during the war, but its
façade was recently restored. The gold-and-white interior is
by the Asam brothers of Munich; Cosmas Damian painted
the frescoes and Egid Quirin executed the stucco-work.

In the chapel built on the spot where Meinrad was killed
is a small Black Madonna; pilgrims come here in the hope
that she will grant their prayers. Gregorian chants sung by
the monks, along with frequent organ concerts, make this an
unforgettable visit. The **Fürstensaal** (Hall of Princes) is
richly appointed, a reminder that before the 15th century the
abbots of Einsiedeln were princes of the German empire.

Today, Einsiedeln is a self-sufficient community of around
100 monks and 50 lay brothers; they work at various trades
ranging from mechanic to stonemason to baker. The monastery
also operates a printing works, a stud farm and a cattle farm.

High in the clouds: the wild Grisons, near Chur

GRISONS

This canton holds three records: it is the biggest, the least populous, and the most polyglot in all Switzerland. It is, in fact, the only canton where three languages are spoken: German (60 percent), Romansh (22 percent) and Italian (13 percent). **Grisons** *(Graubünden, Grischuns, Grigioni)* occupies about one-sixth of the area of the country. This canton's most precious resource is the rough natural beauty it offers to visitors. Its history is closely linked to that of its 10 mountain passes. Even today, several of them remain major arteries of European communication.

The first settlers to leave their mark here were the Rhaetians, whose descendants still speak the Romansh language. In AD15, the Romans, seeking control over the mountain passes, conquered the Rhaetians. Later, the German emperors took it over for the same reason, imposing a feudal system on

Return of the bears

In 2005, Switzerland had its first reported bear sighting in more than 100 years in Grisons. Authorities have been trying to coax brown bears back into Swiss territory from Italy, but they had been unsuccessful until recently. Bears had been hunted to extinction in Switzerland more than a century ago.

the area for centuries. In the 15th century, the peasants organised themselves in associations such as the Grey League (Grauer Bund), which gave its name to the Grisons mountain range. They threw off the yoke of the foreign princes and the Church. External pressure united these solid mountain folk, but they could not remain independent forever. In 1803, after Napoleon's Act of Mediation, they joined the Confederation.

Chur

The gateway to the region, **Chur** *(Coire)* is also the cantonal capital and main crossroads. Westward, you can climb, by way of Flims, to the source of the Rhine; to the south, through the Julier or Albula passes, you can reach St Moritz and other famous ski resorts of Engadine; and to the east lie Davos and Klosters. To get from one valley to the next, you can choose between travelling by car, postal bus and the Rhätische Bahn, the regional narrow-gauge train.

Chur is an active little town. You will love visiting its ancient winding streets and its oddly shaped town squares. To guide you in your wanderings, the local tourist office has organised two walks, marked in an original fashion: just follow the red or green footprints painted on the ground. Both routes leave from the Postplatz and take, respectively, 60 and 75 minutes. In the Poststrasse, the medieval **Rathaus** (town hall) has a lovely courtyard and several beautiful rooms.

The stone steps up the hill past the medieval gates lead to the **Bischöfliches Schloss** (Bishop's Palace), which has been the seat of the bishopric since the Middle Ages. Ahead of you looms the half-Romanesque, half-Gothic **cathedral**, majestic despite its irregular layout (the choir is too high and its axis is misaligned with that of the nave). An immense triptych in gilded woodwork crowns the altar. The treasury, one of the richest in Switzerland, contains many venerable reliquaries.

A fine 17th-century building houses the historical and folk-lore collections of the **Rhätisches Museum** (Rhetic Museum). The **Kunstmuseum** (Fine Arts Museum; open Tues–Sun 10am–5pm, Thur until 8pm; admission fee), on the Postplatz, displays works from the 18th to the 20th century by Grison's artists (Giovanni, Augusto and Alberto Giacometti, and Angelika Kauffman).

Maienfeld (20 minutes from Chur by car) is a lovely village with some attractive bourgeois homes. An excellent red wine is made here, dry and light, and there is no shortage of inns in which to taste it. This is also the land of Heidi, the heroine of the popular children's book by Johanna Spyri.

After visiting Chur, you will find yourself within easy reach of several famous Grisons resorts.

Lenzerheide-Valbella, at 1,500m (4,921ft), draws visitors all year round. **Arosa** (1,740m/5,709 ft) is a charming spot surrounded by forested mountains reflected in

The altar of Chur cathedral

Davos: an Alpine jewel

two small lakes. Sports enthusiasts and romantics will both find what they want in this resort.

As for **Davos** (1,560m/ 5,118ft), its international renown has grown since it began hosting the annual World Economic Forum. But its worldwide pull is not only recent. Thomas Mann made it the setting for his 1924 novel *The Magic Mountain*. Numerous sports facilities and a huge skiing area, shared with **Klosters** (1,180m/ 3,871ft), make this place a jewel not to be missed.

The Vorderrhein

A picturesque route follows the course of the Vorderrhein (Upper Rhine) to its source, near Oberalp pass, on the way to Andermatt and Saint-Gotthard. At **Reichenau**, you enter into the lush green Vorderrhein valley, where the Upper and Lower Rhine unite to form the single great river that flows through Germany and Holland to the North Sea.

Past this small town, the valley narrows and the route rises to the sunny ski town of **Flims** (1,080m/3,545ft), made up of two parts, Flims-Dorf and Flims-Waldhaus; the latter is where you will find the hotels, scattered through a dense forest of pines and larch, interspersed with sparkling lakes. Below Flims is **Laax**, a much smaller town with an interesting baroque church that dates from the end of the 17th century. **Ilanz** proudly calls itself the first city on the Rhine, basing its claims on 1,200 years of history. In **Trun**, visit the impressive 17th-century residence of the abbots of Disentis (now a museum of local art and folklore).

In **Disentis**, the great 12th-century abbey testifies to the importance of this town as a religious centre in the Middle Ages. The current monastery dates from the 17th century, while the baroque abbey church *(Klosterkirche)* was built over the tomb of Sigisbert, the hermit-monk, in the 18th century.

The Hinterrhein

To reach Ticino, you can go through the Hinterrheintal, or valley of the lower Rhine, in the direction of the San Bernardino pass. After the **Domleschg valley**, with its villages and castles, you drive past Thusis to the **Via Mala**: harsh and arid, this canyon carved out by the frothing Rhine is now perfectly accessible. The 'bad way' *(via mala)* opens out onto the Schams (or Schons) valley. The jewel of this

The huge white Benedictine abbey in Disentis

region is **Zillis**, where a 12th-century church harbours the oldest **painted ceiling** in Europe. The 153 panels of St Martin's church were inspired by the New Testament and the lives of Christ and St Martin.

After the endearing village of Andeer, you enter the Rheinwald. **Splügen**, a town favoured by hikers, is also a crossroads: on one side, the Splügen pass leads to Italy; on the other, the San Bernardino pass is the gateway to Ticino.

Engadine

In the valley of the River Inn (or En), which gives **Engadine** its name, the contrast between the ancient villages and the ultramodern resorts is striking. The former are made up of sturdy stone houses with their unique and beautiful *sgraffiti* decorations. This technique consists in covering a dark stucco wall with a white coating, into which a pattern is then scratched in places to reveal the darker layer beneath.

Zernez, in Engadine

Engadine is divided into two regions, lower and upper. The first stretches from Maloja to Zernez. From Chur, you can reach it through the Julier or Albula passes. Lower Engadine extends from Zernez to Martina, on the Austrian border; from Davos or Klosters, you can get here through the Flüela pass.

The village of **Guarda**, in lower Engadine, has preserved its tiny paved streets, its fountains, and its intricately worked houses. If you are curious about local architecture and folklore, be sure to make a stop here. Another very pretty village is **Scuol** (*Schuls* in German), the last stop on the Rhätische Bahn. This dynamic little town, like its neighbours Tarasp and Vulpera, has its own thermal baths.

On the border between lower and upper Engadine, **Zernez** is the main gateway to the **Swiss National Park**. Begin with a visit to the Park House, where you can get all the information you need and also watch an audiovisual presentation on the park. The park itself is small (160 sq km/ 100 sq miles) and very well preserved: you could forget about the human race here, if not for the signs indicating (very clearly) the paths for forest walks. The best time to visit is from mid-June to the end of October, when the Park House is open. The flora is particularly varied because of the very hilly terrain, and you may catch a glimpse of such unusual animals as ibex, elk, marmots and vultures.

The Ofen pass (Fuorn pass/Pass dal Fuorn), just past the park, takes you to **Müstair** ('monastery' in Romansh), the main village of the wooded valley of the same name, situated at the Italian border. During the Reformation, the towns of the region converted to Protestantism, but Müstair, barricaded behind the walls of its monastery, remained Catholic. Here, Romansh is king.

At the end of the village, the **Abbey of St John the Baptist** was founded in the 8th century by a Bishop of Chur who was related to Charlemagne. (Tradition has it that Charlemagne himself was responsible for its foundation.) The church, with its triple apse, underwent transformations in the 15th century. The wall paintings are some of the finest remaining examples of the Carolingian period (the first half of the 9th century). Also, note the 12th-century statue of Charlemagne.

Back in the Inn valley, stop at **Zuoz**, a quaint, well-preserved town. It has a church with windows by Giacometti and a group of typical Engadine houses around the main square that date from the 16th to 18th century.

St Moritz, a world-renowned ski resort, attracts a rich and cosmopolitan clientele. The success of St Moritz – the birthplace of Alpine winter sports in 1884 – is justified by its favoured natural setting, dry and sunny climate, elaborate recreational facilities and a carefully maintained reputation for elegance. This region, a paradise of snow sports, offers infinite possibilities. Its bobsled and skeleton slopes are very famous *(see page 130)*. The village is roughly divided into two parts: St Moritz-Bad, where the thermal baths are located, and, on the hill, St Moritz-Dorf, with its palatial hotels.

Worthy of note are two museums: the **Engadine Museum** (furniture, tile stoves and historic weapons through the ages) and the **Segantini Museum**, which has landscapes by the Italian painter Giovanni Segantini inspired by views of the Engadine region.

Northeast of St Moritz, ride the funicular to **Muottas Muragl**, a panoramic vista point from which you can survey all of the upper Engadine. See if you can spot Pontresina, the lakes of St Moritz and Silvaplana, and Sils (where Nietzsche

Glacier Express

There's no excuse for missing the Glacier Express (<www.glacier express.ch>) that links St Moritz to Zermatt. This 7½-hour railway trip across the Alps, ending at the Oberalp pass, is spellbinding. Panoramic windows in each railway carriage offer an exciting spectacle both in winter and in summer. The train goes through 91 tunnels, crosses 291 bridges and takes hairpin turns that will leave you with goosebumps.

The Bernina Range, from Morteratsch on the Glacier Express

stayed while writing *Thus Spoke Zarathustra*). Even further out is the Maloja pass. Or climb higher to the Piz Nair (3,057m/10,030ft), reachable by funicular, then cable car, and finally by foot (15 minutes).

Pontresina (1,803m/5,915ft), on the Bernina Pass road, has some beautiful ski slopes. A base for alpinists – you will find the largest climbing school in Switzerland here – it offers hiking trails as well. The glacier trail at Morteratsch has signs explaining the formation of moraines, deposits of earth and stone left by moving glaciers.

Whether you go through the Bernina Pass in a car, train or bus, you will never forget the sights afforded by this route into the Poschiavo Valley: the Morteratsch glacier, the **Diavolezza** panorama, the Piz Palü and, on the other side of the pass, the Alpine garden of Alp Grüm. In this valley, Italian is spoken; in fact, all over Poschiavo, you can sense the Mediterranean atmosphere.

Ascona's charming waterfront

TICINO

When you arrive in **Ticino** from Grisons, you suddenly find yourself in the thick of Italian conversation, music and food, basking in a sunny and charming atmosphere that seems to have been lifted straight out of neighbouring Italy. Tourists are drawn here by the picturesque villages and lakes, the deep valleys that take you back to another age, the many cultural offerings, and a dazzling array of outdoor activities, including walking, sailing and skiing.

Ticino is closer to Milan than it is to Bern, and its ties to Italy, especially the cultural ones, are very strong. Ticino was torn from the Milanese by the Swiss in the 15th century and dominated by the cantons on the other side of the Saint Gotthard pass until 1803, when it was made a canton of its own. This attachment to the Confederation is all the more remarkable given that, until the end of the 19th century – that is, until the construction of the Gotthard railway tunnel – the canton spent every winter cut off from the rest of Switzerland. The road tunnel was not finished until 1980.

Bellinzona

The capital of Ticino, **Bellinzona** guards the way to three mountain passes – Saint Gotthard, Lukmaier and San Bernardino – which explains the town's turbulent history. It was a coveted location, fought over by the Romans, the Franks, the Lombards and the Swiss of the Confederation.

Beautiful Lombard-style arches, pastel-coloured houses with balconies, and old churches make up the heart of Bellinzona. Not to be missed are the three medieval castles surrounded by **crenellated walls**.

The **Castel Grande** (open Mon 10am–6pm, Tues–Sun 9am–10pm; admission fee; you can buy a combination ticket for all three castles) or Castel Vecchio, dating originally from the 4th century AD, has been creatively restored by the architect Aurelio Galfetti. This group of buildings includes a historical museum, theatres and two restaurants. The second, the **Castello di Montebello** (open daily 8am–8pm; admission fee), was built from the 13th to the 15th century. It was restored in 1903 (exterior) and during the 1970s (interior). A museum of archaeology and history, the Museo Civico, has been installed here: it displays pieces found in archaeological digs all over the canton. The third castle, which towers above

Castel Grande, the oldest and largest of Bellinzona's castles the two others, is the 15th-century **Castello di Sasso Corbaro** (open Easter–Oct Mon 10am–6pm, Tues–Sun 10am–10pm; admission fee). It was built in some six months of day and night labour by order of the Duke of Milan, who feared an imminent offensive by the Swiss. Bellinzona's three fortresses are often called by their nicknames – Uri, Schwyz and Unterwald – in memory of the baillifs sent by the *Waldstätten* in the 16th century to rule over the region.

Locarno and Lake Maggiore

West of Bellinzona, on Lake Maggiore, **Locarno** luxuriates in a warm and sunny climate, with orange trees, banana plants and palm trees growing in abundance year-round.

Madonna del Sasso

The best-known monument in Locarno is the **Madonna del Sasso**, five minutes from the centre of town by funicular. For centuries, pilgrims have climbed the steep path to its sanctuary. The church, which is perched on a rocky cliff, seems immense from a distance, but this impression lessens upon entering, perhaps because of the huge number of artworks that are housed inside it.

From here hikers and, in winter, skiers can take the cable car up the steep flanks of Mount Cardada, a trip of just a few minutes. A ski lift takes you the rest of the way to the **Cimetta** (1,671m/ 5,482ft), a superb belvedere, where the view of lake and town is truly breathtaking.

Once back 'on land', those who love art and history should make a point of visiting the **Castello Visconti**, which was partially restored in the 1920s. The arch-lined 15th-century courtyard bears witness to the lost splendour of the castle's fortifications. Within the castle is the Museo Civico, a rich archaeological collection with many relics that date as far back as the Roman Empire (open Apr–Oct Tues–Sun 10am–noon, 2–5pm; admission fee).

Follow the Via Rusca to the **Piazza Grande**, the main square of Locarno, lined with shops and cafés, which hosts the screenings and ceremonies of the **International Film Festival** each August (<www.pardo.ch>).

Up the hill, the **Città Vecchia** (Old Town) has an appeal-ing combination of stately villas, time-worn tenements, hid-

Modern Architecture

Lugano, like Bellinzona, Locarno, and other cities in Ticino, has many excellent examples of modern architecture. In fact, since the end of the 1960s, Ticino has seen the development of several generations of talented architects, whose international renown has inspired local authorities to invest in sizeable architectural undertakings. (A detailed and interesting history of this phenomenon, entitled *Discovering Modern Architecture in the Ticino*, is available from tourist offices throughout the canton.)

Examples include a series of creations by Mario Botta: the Banca del Gottardo (1988, viale Stefano Franscini), the Palazzo Telecom (1997 in Bellinzona) and the Palazzo Botta (1991, via Ciani 16, Lugano). Also of note are the Architect's Studio (1994 in Mendrisio) by Ivano Gianola and the Palazzo delle Pose (1996 in Locarno) by Livio Vacchini.

den gardens and venerable churches. The Casa Rusca, on the Piazza Sant Antonio, contains works from the collection of Jean Arp (who died in Locarno in 1966), a leading Surrealist and one of the founders of the Dadaist art movement, as well as other donations.

Lake Maggiore *(Lago Maggiore)*, shared by Italy and Switzerland, is popular with excursionists and lovers of water sports. The **Isles of Brissago** make a fun day trip. On San Pancrazio, the largest, is the **Botanical Garden**, devoted to exotic plants – bamboo, sugar cane, cactus – and all manner of citrus trees. Some boats continue toward Stresa to the Borromeo Islands, in Italian waters.

Ascona is separated from Locarno only by the mouth of the River Maggia. Once a simple fishing village, this fashionable little town has long played host to artists and intellectuals: Isadora Duncan, Paul Klee and Lenin all stayed here. Also contributing to its fame are the frequent art exhibitions that are hosted here and an annual jazz festival (<www.jazzascona.ch>).

From Locarno or Ascona, a day trip is enough to explore the surrounding high, isolated valleys. If you're in good shape, you can explore the valleys on foot (maps of walking trails are available in tourist offices); alternatively, you can travel by car or postal bus. The wild and magnificent **Val Verzasca**, will not fail to move you. The most remote village, **Sonogno**, is only 31km (19 miles) from Locarno, but the contrast between it and the luxurious prosperity of the lakeside could not be more striking. The simple houses of Sonogno are entirely constructed of dry stones balanced one on another without any mortar.

The **Valle Maggia** follows the meandering River Maggia, northeast of Ascona and Locarno. Italianate architecture in all its variations is universal here – until you reach the wooden chalets of the remote village of **Bosco** *(Gurin)*, in a side valley settled in the 12th century by emigrants from the canton of Valais. Their descendants still speak an obscure Swiss-German dialect that is unique in Ticino.

The **Centovalli**, which links Locarno with Domodossola, is delightfully twisty, while the Onsernone valley is rough but authentic nonetheless.

Lugano and its Lake

First town of Ticino, **Lugano** sweeps gently down between two mountains and slopes to a shaded lakefront promenade. Yachts and tourist boats ply the lake, while pleasant villages cling to jagged outcroppings along its shore.

Here, the sun shines for more than 2,000 hours each year. Forsythias and mimosas blossom in February; March is the time for camellias, magnolias and peach trees; while April glows with azaleas, rhododendrons, wisteria and Japanese

Lugano, the most alluring of Ticino's lake resorts

cherry trees in bloom. The main square, **Piazza della Riforma**, is a vast space devoted to row upon row of café tables; you can linger here indefinitely, sipping an espresso or an aperitif. Covered shopping streets filled with boutiques lead from the plaza into the old town.

Facing the lake at the southern end of the Via Nassa is the tiny church of **Santa Maria degli Angioli** (St Mary of the Angels), with the finest Renaissance frescoes in Ticino. The most famous cycle, painted at the beginning of the 16th century, is a luminous *Passion of Christ* by Bernardino Luini, a student of Leonardo da Vinci; the same artist also decorated one of the side chapels.

Along the lake, the beautifully landscaped Parco Civico can provide a quiet respite with a display of flowers that is changed often to reflect the different seasons. Art lovers can visit the Fine Arts Museum in the Villa Ciani in the

Piazza della Riforma, Lugano's main square

park (open Tues–Sun 10am–noon, 2–6pm; admission fee) to see some outstanding temporary exhibitions (whilst the museum's permanent collection is being relocated). The **Cantonal Art Museum** (open Tues 2–5pm, Wed–Sun 10am–5pm; admission fee), occupying three buildings built between the 15th and 19th centuries at Via Canova 10, also hosts exhibitions by contemporary artists in addition to its permanent collection.

An enthusiastic journalist once called Lugano 'the Rio of Europe'. For him, Mount San Salvatore was nothing less than a little brother of the Sugarloaf. To see if he was right, take a look – the best view is from **Mount Brè** (accessible by funicular; <www.montebre.ch>). San Salvatore itself (912m/2,992ft) can be reached by funicular as well, for fabulous views and pleasant hiking trails back to the town.

A cruise on the lake will let you marvel at the peaks surrounding it and to see, or stop and visit, some quaint villages.

Gandria. Many artists have been attracted to this fishing village covered in flowers, yet Gandria, located northeast of Lugano, has never lost its authenticity.

Melide, south of Lugano, can be reached by land or water. Since 1959, millions have come to this village to lose themselves in the labyrinthine world of **Swissminiatur** (open daily mid-Mar–mid-Nov 9am–6pm; admission fee; <www.swissminiatur.ch>), a model built to 1:25 scale of more than 100 national monuments. Trains glide on their tracks through tunnels and mountains, funiculars scale the peaks and boats drift by… the exhibition is fascinating and complete down to the last detail.

Morcote is an adorable village nestled into a hill. A long stone staircase from the 17th century takes you up a steep slope to the medieval chapel of Saint-Antoine. Further up, a slender belltower marks the **church of Santa Maria del Sasso** and its cemetery, full of towering cypress trees.

Side by side: two Swiss icons

VALAIS

Since prehistoric times, the long, wide, untamed valley that bears the name of **Valais** (*Wallis* in German) has been an important means of communication between northern and southern as well as eastern and western Europe. In fact, Valais is really a continuation of the Rhône Valley; that great river, beginning as a melted glacier, finally empties its waters into Lake Geneva.

Here nature defies the imagination: waterfalls drop down the sheerest of cliffs while glaciers blind you with their whiteness. There are orchards in full bloom, rugged vineyards, mythical summits and cowbells tinkling in the mountain pastures. The mountains to the north protect the valley against cold winds and often rain, while the orientation of the side valleys to the *Föhn* (a characteristic warm, dry wind) gives the region a gentle climate.

Each of the adjacent valleys has its own customs and traditions. Halfway into Valais, somewhere around Sierre, the French language gives way to Swiss-German. But the linguistic division and cultural diversity of this canton doesn't seem to prevent the cohesion of its inhabitants, who are united by a strong Catholic faith.

After its domination by the Romans, Valais was controlled by the Burgundians. During the 15th century, the King of Burgundy bequeathed it to the bishops of Sion, whose influence made it impermeable to the Protestant

Reformation. But there was no resisting the occupation by France after the Revolution in 1798. Made its own independent state by Bonaparte, Valais became a French *département* – known as Simplon – before finally joining the Confederation in 1815.

We will survey the length of this valley, rich in churches and monasteries, from Saint-Maurice to the sources of the Rhône, losing ourselves from time to time in the valleys along the side.

Lower Valais

Above Monthey, **Champéry** (1,050m/3,445ft) offers lovers of winter sports access to a huge ski domain, **Portes du Soleil**, which reaches all the way to France. In summer, more than 200km (125 miles) of groomed slopes await the eager mountain biker.

St Bernards

The famous St Bernard dogs are synonymous with Switzerland and her mountains. At a hospice, located at the Grand St Bernard Pass, these iconic dogs have been bred since the 18th century. A line of monks beginning with Bernard of Menthon have inhabited the hospice since the 11th century and still live on the site (guests can stay there, but the accommodation is modest). This idyllic location, right on the Italian-Swiss border, has a museum about the pass and the famous dogs, plus a kennel. The monks recently sold the kennel to a private foundation, but the dogs can still be visited here during the summer months when the pass is open (approximately June–early October). In winter, the dogs can be visited at a new kennel in the town of Martigny, not far from the pass. Every year a limited number of St Bernard puppies can be bought for around 2,000 Swiss Francs each. Call 027 722 6542 for visiting times or visit <www.fondation-barry.ch> for further information.

The Abbaye de St-Maurice

Back in the main valley, stop at the town of **Saint Maurice**, wedged between a precipitous cliff and a mountain range. The **Abbaye de Saint-Maurice** is among the oldest monastic institutions in Christendom. For nearly 14 centuries monks, and later canons, have been singing their psalms here. All this fervour commemorates Maurice, a Christian officer of the Roman Army who, because he had refused to worship the Roman gods, was massacred with his followers, some 6,000 men, around the year 285.

Since the 4th century, pilgrims (among them princes of Christendom) have come to place their offerings on the martyrs' tombs. These accumulated gifts make up the **treasury**, which includes some exceptional pieces of silversmith work.

Martigny, located at a sharp angle along the Rhône riverbank, has long been an important crossroads. Its old town contains the ruins of a Roman amphitheatre, which could hold 6,000 spectators. On a fortification to the west stands the Bâtiaz, the stark tower (now restored) of a 13th-century castle. Finally, outside the centre of town, an audacious architectural complex is home to the **Pierre-Gianadda Foundation** (open daily Jun–Nov 9am–7pm, Nov–Jun 10am–6pm; admission fee; <www.gianadda.ch>), which brings together a museum of Roman antiquities, an automobile museum and a cultural centre that organises high-quality temporary exhibitions (Gauguin, Modigliani, Picasso) as well as concerts and theatre programmes. The park is full of statues by Rodin, Brancusi, Miró, Moore, Dubuffet and more.

If you are hurrying to get across the Alps you can take the train or drive along the E27 with its almost 6-km (4-mile) long tunnel that connects Switzerland and Italy. By doing this you will avoid the difficult road that runs across the **Grand St Bernard Pass** (2,740m/8,100ft high) and which is closed all winter. But it also means you'll miss the famous **hospice** founded by Saint Bernard of Menthon. There is a museum here which is full of artifacts from Napoleon's passage through the pass, with 40,000 men on their way to the battle of Marengo in 1800. In the kennel, friendly St Bernard dogs are raised and trained to rescue avalanche victims *(see page 93)*.

Sion and Environs

Nearly 1,000 years ago, when bishop-princes held sovereign authority over the whole of Valais, **Sion** added a politico-religious role to its traditional military one. The most famous of its bishops, Cardinal Matthew Schiner (1465–1522), is still the hero of the canton, even though his schemes – he pushed the then-young Confederation to ally itself with the Pope, sending it into war with the King of France – finally led to the defeat of the Swiss at Marignano.

Sion, the capital of Valais, is overlooked by two imposing hills. The first, Tourbillon, the hill closest to the mountains, is crowned by the ruins of a 13th-century episcopal castle. The second, Valère, closer to the river and the centre of town, supports an imposing fortified church (open Tues–Sat 10am–5pm, Sun 2–5pm; admission fee). This Romanesque-Gothic structure, once the cathedral of Sion, is known for its naïve stone carving, 15th-century frescoes, and choir stalls from the 17th century. The organ, constructed at the beginning of the 10th century, is one of the oldest functioning organs in Europe.

Between the hills, in Rue des Châteaux, there are two more museums of interest: **La Majorie** (open Jun–Sept Tues–Sun 1–6pm, Oct–May Tues–Sun 1–5pm; admission fee), once the residence of church officials, now holds the Musée Cantonal des Beaux-Arts (Cantonal Fine Arts Museum); and the modern **Musée Cantonal d'Archéologie** (Cantonal Museum of Archaeology; open Jun–Sept Tues–Sun 10am–noon, 1–6pm, Oct–May Tues–Sun 1–5pm; admission fee), on the other side of the street, which brings together objects found at archaeological digs all over the canton.

In the heart of town, you will see the 17th-century town hall, painted pink; the astronomical belfry clock is from 1667. The **cathedral** (Notre-Dame-du-Glarier), in late Gothic style, was built after a fire destroyed the original Romanesque edifice, whose belltower is all that remains.

Sion is a good starting point for day trips to the neighbouring ski resorts. To the north, **Crans-Montana** offers exceptional ski slopes; it also has facilities for tennis and golf, and various places to shop. Food-lovers will not be disappointed with the cuisine, and night-crawlers may run into holidaying celebrities.

To the south, the **Val d' Herens** is known for its pic-

Swiss pyramids

The Val d'Herens, southeast of Sion, contains a relic from the Ice Age: the so-called Pyramides d'Euseigne (*below*), earth pillars protected from erosion by the flat stones which cap them.

Traditional Valaisian barns at Ayer in the Val d'Anniviers

turesque villages with dark wood chalets, generously hung with red geraniums in summer. **Evolène** is an authentic old village, and **Arolla** (2,000m/6,562ft), to the south, is a centre for mountain climbing.

At the bottom of the Hérémence valley, the 285-m (935-ft) tall **Grande Dixence dam** was the tallest dam in the world until 1980. You can arrange to visit from mid-June to September (tel: 027 328 43 11; <www.grande-dixence.ch>).

Continuing down the Rhône to the east, you will reach the last bastion of the French language, announced by a sign in two languages: **Sierre/Siders**. Surrounded by vineyards, the town enjoys a particularly dry climate. Taste vintage wines in any one of a number of cellars, or learn about viticultural techniques in the **Valaisian Museum of Wines and Wine-making** (open Apr–Nov Tues–Fri 2–5pm; admission fee).

On a detour to the south of Sierre, nestled in the **Val d'Anniviers**, you'll find **Chandolin** (1,935m/6,345ft), one

Leukerbad's baths

With six public baths and a number of hotels offering their own thermal bathing options, Leukerbad (<www.leukerbad.ch>) is an ideal location for relaxation. The temperature at the source is 51°C (124°F), and about 3.9 million litres (860,000 gallons) of natural hot water flows daily into the private and public baths, giving this area the largest amount of thermal water in all of Europe.

of the highest European villages that is inhabited year round, as well as a few other charming mountain resorts, including St-Luc, Grimentz and Zinal, all of which are dwarfed by two mountains: Mount Weisshorn (4,505m/ 14,780 ft) and the Zinalrothorn (4,220m/13,848ft).

Past Sierre, in the Rhône valley, **Leuk** *(Loèche)* can be recognised by its castles and towers dating from the era of the 'majors' (church officials of Sion). The road that runs through the Gemmi Pass, leading to Kandersteg (Bernese Oberland), leaves from **Leukerbad** *(Loèche-les-Bains)*, an upland spa and centre for hiking and mountain climbing.

From Gampel, approximately halfway between Sierre and Brig, a road leads steeply to **Lötschental**, a high, wild valley which was unreachable in winter for centuries. That is, until 1913, when the 15-km (10-mile) long rail tunnel that links Valais to the Bernese Oberland was inaugurated. Pull over in **Kippel** and stroll around the church. The **Lötschentaler Museum** reveals the secrets of this mysterious valley.

Upper Valais

The most famous mountain in Valais, the **Matterhorn** (*Mont Cervin/Monte Cervino*, 4,480m/14,690ft) is, if not the highest in the Alps, certainly the most impressive. This formidable horn-shaped peak has never ceased to be a challenge to mountaineers the world over.

The first expedition to reach the top was led by a young Englishman, Edward Whymper. His team scaled the northeastern face of the mountain. But the conquest, on 14 July 1865, did little to dispel the terror that the Matterhorn has always inspired. On the contrary, it reinforced it: on their descent, four of Whymper's six companions fell to their deaths.

The **Alpine Museum** in **Zermatt** retraces the history of the conquest of the Matterhorn. This famous resort town has often served as a base for Alpine expeditions. From Visp *(Viège)* in the Rhône Valley, head up the Mattertal (37km/23 miles) to arrive at the resort, where cars are prohibited and sleds, carriages and electric carts are the sole means of transport. (Cars have to stop at the village of Täsch where there is ample parking. Trains run every 20 minutes during the day to Zermatt.) Zermatt offers comfortable lodgings and high-altitude skiing year round. A cogwheel railway will take you

Mountaineers' graves, Zermatt

to **Gornergrat** (3,135m/10,285ft; <www.gornergrat.ch>), with an unforgettable view of **Mount Rose**.

If you're not afraid of heights, take the four successive cable cars to the **Little Matterhorn**: the fourth, overlooking the glacier, deposits you at the highest ski resort in Europe (3,820m/12,533ft).

In a parallel valley nestles another famous resort, **Saas-Fee**, dominated by several mountains topping 4,000m (13,100ft). Cars are not permitted (you may park in a special area provided at the entrance). A subway links Fleskinn to Mittelallalin, 3,500m (11,483ft) up, where the **Ice Palace** awaits you (<www.eispavillon.ch>). In a cave of

The cog railway to Gornergrat, with the Matterhorn beyond

more than 5,000 cu m (16,400 cu ft), you can discover the secrets of 1,000-year-old glaciers.

Although the Swiss have mixed feelings towards Napoleon, **Brig** has nonetheless named one of its streets after the great man. He built the Simplon Pass road, which begins here, through the Alps. This town is dominated by the three onion-shaped domes of the **Stockalper Castle**, built by Kaspar Jodok von Stockalper (1609–91), a very wealthy businessman. The **Simplon Pass** (2,005m/6,578ft), only 25km (16 miles) away, is the high point of a spectacular road, all gorges and steep embankments, which winds its way into Italy.

Heading back north-east up the Rhône Valley is the summer and winter sports resort of Bettmeralp (<www.bettmer alp.ch>). This region serves as an excellent launching point to see the **Aletsch glacier**, the longest in Switzerland. At the furthest point of the Rhône Valley, which is called Goms Valley after the town of Fiesch, is the **Furka Pass**. At 2,430m (7,976ft), it is a vital link between the east and the west of Switzerland and offers an incomparable view on to the peaks of the Bernese Oberland. Just before the pass, you can stop for a close look at the **Rhône glacier**, as impressive as any you'll see in Switzerland. The **ice cave** is open from June to October.

GENEVA

Geneva is Switzerland's second largest city after Zurich and capital of the tiny canton of the same name. It is far more cosmopolitan than any other Swiss city – not just because of its location right next to the French border but also because it is the base of numerous international organisations as well as European seat of the United Nations. The population is just as diverse; approximately 40 percent are foreigners.

Geneva's location at the western tip of Lake Geneva has been considered a strategic one since 58BC, when Julius Caesar and his troops destroyed the ancient bridge over the Rhône to halt the movement of Helvetian troops toward Gaul. Since then, many a sovereign has coveted Geneva as a communications nexus and a centre of trade. Thus, the city has been under the control of the dukes of Burgundy, the German emperor, the dukes of Savoy and, briefly, Napoleon Bonaparte.

In 1602, several thousand mercenaries brought in by the Duke of Savoy besieged the city. Taking advantage of a particularly dark night, they scaled the city walls, but the spears wielded by Geneva's men, along with the boiling soup hurled by its women, got the better of them. Each year around 11 December, the *Escalade* (Scaling of the Walls) is commemorated by a torchlight procession and a series of masked balls.

The French theologian Jean Calvin made Geneva a great centre of Protestantism, and from 1541 Protestant refugees and pilgrims flowed into the 'Protestant Rome'. Today, tolerance reigns. The city is the seat of the ecumenical World Council of Churches and contains several Protestant, Catholic and Orthodox churches, a synagogue and a mosque.

In 1920, American president Woodrow Wilson made Geneva the world capital of diplomacy by choosing it to be the seat for the League of Nations. The city, which had so long been a centre for banking and watchmaking, was thrust onto the world stage, and since then numerous international agencies, including the International Committee of the Red Cross (ICRC), the World Health Organization (WHO), the World Trade Organisation (WTO) and the European Free Trade Association (EFTA) have chosen Geneva as their home.

A Stroll Through the City

The tallest monument in Geneva and a symbol of the city, the **Water Jet** *(Jet d'Eau)* is visible from many parts of town: its jet of water reaches the height of a 40-storey building.

The imposing Mont-Blanc bridge links the two parts of town. Here, you will see the sudden narrowing at the spot where the lake becomes a powerful river: the Rhône, which enters the lake at one end and exits at the other. From the bridge on the right bank, Mont Blanc can often be seen peeking out from the French Alps to the south. To the west of the

The *Jet d'Eau* has become a symbol of Geneva

The imposing Grand Théâtre

bridge is Rousseau Island, accessible on foot by the Bergues bridge. The statue facing the lake is of writer and philosopher Jean-Jacques Rousseau (1712–78). Downstream, the river is split in two by what the Genevans call simply the Island. Only a watchtower remains of the castle built here in 1219.

At the other side of the bridge you enter the luxurious **shopping district**. Wander down the rue du Rhône, the rue de la Confédération, the rue du Marché, the rue de la Croix-d'Or and the rue de la Corraterie – an elegant boulevard that ends at the place Neuve. Three impressive buildings are here: the **Grand Théâtre** (inspired by the Opéra Garnier in Paris), the **Conservatoire de Musique** and the **Musée Rath**, a sublime Greek-style structure constructed in 1826 as the first fine-arts museum in Switzerland.

Place Neuve opens into the tree-lined promenade des Bastions. On the left is the **Reformation Monument**. Erected in 1909, the 400th anniversary of the birth of Calvin, this 100-m (330-ft) long wall bears religious inscriptions in several languages. The group of sculptures at the centre represents Calvin and the French reformers Théodore de Bèze and Guillaume Farel as well as the Scottish preacher John Knox. Facing the monument is the main building of the **University of Geneva**, which is the offspring of Calvin's Theological Academy.

The Old City

The Old City is a maze of streets and historic dwellings. If you take the rue Saint-Léger at the end of the promenade des Bastions, you will arrive at the **place du Bourg-de-Four**, with its attractive fountain, surrounded by the Palais de Justice (1712) and some lovely houses (16th–18th centuries). Occupying the highest point in the Old City is the **Cathédrale Saint-Pierre**. This has been a place of worship of some kind since pagan antiquity. In the 12th century, its construction began first in the Romanesque and later in the Gothic style. In the 18th century, the façade was adorned with classical columns that still provoke controversy today. The interior is as austere as the doctrine Calvin preached here for more than 20 years. From the top of the northern tower (take the lift), there's an exceptional **view** of Geneva and surrounding areas.

Just around the corner from the cathedral is a new museum devoted to the Reformation, **Musée International de la Réforme** (open Tues–Sun 10am–5pm; admission fee; <www.musee-reforme.ch>). With films, rare books and manuscripts, the importance of Geneva is tied into the overall history of the Reformation.

The **Tavel House** (the Museum of Old Geneva; open Tues–Sun 10am–5pm; free), on the rue du Puits-Saint-Pierre, is the oldest dwelling in Geneva. On the corner of the rue de l'Hôtel-de-Ville, be sure to notice the **Arsenal**, with a line-up of 17th- and 18th-century cannon under its arches. The three wall mosaics, dating from 1949, represent important episodes in the city's history. On the other side of the street, the **Hôtel de Ville** (town hall), seat of the cantonal government, has an elegant Renaissance courtyard where concerts can be heard in summer. In this building, the Geneva Convention, the first convention agreement on the treatment of prisoners of war, was signed in 1864.

Rousseau's birthplace

Just past the Hôtel de Ville, follow the picturesque **Grand-Rue**, lined with buildings from the 15th to the 18th century; one of them, No. 34, was once the workshop of the painter Ferdinand Hodler. A little further down, No. 40 is the birthplace of Rousseau. A small museum, **Espace Rousseau**, devoted to his life is located here (open Tues–Sun 11am–5.30pm; admission fee). Parallel to this street, the **rue des Granges**, a bastion of the great bourgeois families of Geneva, distinguishes itself by its beautiful Louis XVI-style houses.

International City

The vast **Palais des Nations** (tours Apr–Oct daily 10am–noon, 2–4pm, Jul–Aug daily 10am–5pm; Nov–Mar Mon–Fri 10am– noon, 2–4pm; admission fee; <www.unog.ch>), conceived as the headquarters of the League of Nations, was inaugurated in 1937, with the spectre of war already looming over attempts at international cooperation. After World War II, the newly gathered United Nations claimed the building, at the heart of Ariana Park, as its European headquarters. Guided tours take you through the historic rooms, notably the Council Hall, which has remarkable frescoes, the enormous Assembly Hall, and a peek at one of the conference rooms.

For a moving look at the history of the Red Cross, visit the **Musée International de la Croix-Rouge et du Croissant-Rouge** (open Wed–Mon 10am–5pm; admission fee;

<www.micr.ch>), next door to the Palais des Nations, for an understanding of the important work of the organisation from its beginnings to the present day.

Parks and Gardens

Geneva is rightly proud of its huge parks, with their fountains, sculptures, pavilions and cafés. The **English Garden**, on the left bank, is known mainly for its giant floral clock, 5m/16ft in diameter, whose immense face is made up of thousands of flowers and plants, replanted twice each year. The clock symbolises Geneva's watchmaking industry. By the water, you will also find boats that leave to many destinations along the lake, including some in France.

On the right bank, Geneva's most pompous monument, the mausoleum of the Duke of Brunswick (1804–73), presides over the **Jardin Brunswick** (Brunswick Garden) on quai

The International Committee of the Red Cross headquarters

du Mont-Blanc. The duke, who spent his last years in exile in Geneva, left his immense fortune to the city on the condition that a mausoleum be erected in his honour.

A mythical spot in Geneva is the **Bains des Paquis** (Paquis baths), dating from 1932 and recently renovated. This natural swimming pool is built at the port on the right side.

After crossing the **Mon-Repos** and **Perle du Lac** parks bordering the lake, you will arrive at the **Botanical Garden**. This ensemble brings together greenhouses filled with tropical plants, a pond filled with aquatic vegetation, an arboretum, a rock garden covered in mountain plants and an aviary.

Geneva's Museums

Geneva is a very active city, both culturally and artistically, and is particularly rich in museums, foundations and galleries. At the **Musée d'Histoire Naturelle** (Museum of Natural History; open Tues–Sun 9.30am–5pm; free), you can traverse 2km (about 1 mile) of corridors on several levels, viewing some 3,000 species of mammal and marine life. The birds are accompanied by samples of birdsong.

The most important of Geneva's museums is the **Musée d'Art et d'Histoire** (Museum of Art and History; open Tues–Sun 10am–5pm; free). The painting department contains works by Dutch, Flemish, French and Swiss masters. The most precious work here is the altarpiece from St Peter's Cathedral, painted by Konrad Witz in 1444. Entitled *La Pêche Miraculeuse* (The Miracle of the Fishes), this painting is the first in art history to repre-

CERN

The European Centre for Nuclear Research (CERN; tours available, reservations needed; <www.cern.ch>), on Geneva's northern outskirts, is the world centre for particle physics research. Guides explain CERN's work and take visitors to see the antimatter factory or one of the particle accelerators.

Inside the Musée d'Art Moderne et Contemporain

sent an identifiable landscape. It features Christ walking on the waters of the port of Geneva. Important temporary exhibitions organised by the Museum of Art and History are presented at the **Musée Rath** *(see page 104)*.

The **Centre d'Art Contemporain** (open Tues–Sun 11am–6pm; admission fee) offers temporary exhibitions of new experimental artists, performances and also film screenings. The former factory for the Geneva Society for Physics Instruments is now the headquarters for the **Musée d'Art Moderne et Contemporain** (MAMCO; open Tues–Fri noon–6pm, Sat–Sun 11am–6pm; admission fee), with 4,000 sq m (13,120 sq ft) of surface area devoted to widely varying exhibitions.

The **Patek Philippe Museum** (near the Plainpalais at 7 rue des Vieux-Grenadiers; open Tues–Fri 2–6pm, Sat 10am–6pm; admission fee; <www.patekmuseum.com>) displays a collection of watches dating back to the 16th century and has a workshop where you can see a master watchmaker in action.

VAUD AND LAKE GENEVA

In the canton of **Vaud**, the most populous in western Switzerland, French is spoken, mixed with the rural dialect of the region. Two mountain ranges, the Alps and the Jura, surround Vaud, providing wide variations of landscapes and climate. To the south, the Lake of Geneva *(Lac Léman)* – the largest of the Alpine lakes – has two-thirds of its waters in Swiss territory and the other third in France. Lake Geneva has always fascinated artists, poets and composers. As peaceful as it seems most of the time, with sailing boats, steamers and motorboats, elegant swans and carefree ducks, this miniature ocean can unleash the occasional tempest throwing huge waves against the shores of the crescent-shaped lake.

In summer, vacationers and Vaud natives politely compete for space on the café terraces; small glasses of the local white wine are emptied as fast as they can be refilled.

La Côte

With a view across Lake Geneva to the French Alps, the villages of **La Côte** are dotted along the 60km (37 miles) of lake shore from the edge of Geneva eastwards to the busy university and commercial city of Lausanne. If you drive from town to town, take the lake road that is parallel to the water rather than the motorway further inland. Beyond Nyon begins the wine-growing region of La Côte. You can follow the signposted Route du Vignoble (Route of the Vineyards) up gently terraced hillsides. Some highlights to visit along the coast:

Coppet evokes the memory of a great writer, Germaine Necker, better known as Madame de Staël. Her father, Jacques Necker, a Genevan banker who was named Director General of Finance under Louis XVI, acquired the **château** (today a museum) in 1784. When Madame de Staël fled

Napoleon's Paris in 1803, she exiled herself to Coppet, where she surrounded herself with a court of her own: Benjamin Constant, Madame de Récamier and Chateaubriand. One of her friends reported that 'more wit is dispensed in one day at Coppet than in one year anywhere else in the world'.

In the town centre of **Nyon** is the **Musée Romain** (Roman Museum; open summer Tues–Sun 10am–noon, 2–6pm; winter Tues–Sun 2–6pm; admission fee; <www.mrn.ch>), which houses the ruins of a Roman basilica, as well as remains and artifacts of Roman life in the area.

The five-towered **château** (open Tues–Sun Apr–Oct 10am–5pm, Nov–Mar 2–5pm; free) of Nyon served as a bastion for the dukes of Savoy, who expanded their domain from the other side of the lake. In the courtyard, a Romanesque mosaic recalls that Nyon was founded by Julius Caesar around 45BC. The château contains a collection of pretty Nyon porcelain,

Nyon's Musée Romain houses local archaeological finds

Fireworks at the Paléo Festival

which dates from the late 18th and early 19th centuries. Near the château, on the rue Maupertuis, the vestiges of a Roman basilica from the 1st century AD stand next to a small museum full of Roman objects found here and elsewhere in the region.

In April, Nyon welcomes the international documentary film festival Visions du Réel, while in July, during the **Paléo Festival** (<www.paleo.ch>) a wave of musical madness descends on Nyon. This French-speaking Woodstock (previously the Nyon Folk Festival) brings together many musical styles and trends.

Rolle is endowed with a 13th-century castle on the banks of the lake. The inhabitants of Bern, who invaded the canton of Vaud in the 16th century, burned it down twice.

Morges makes its reputation in spring, when the annual Tulip Festival is held here. No less than 300,000 of these flowers are displayed in Independence Park, near the lake. Before the construction of the railway, Morges was an important port for the ferrymen of the lake.

The imposing **château** on the port was erected in the 13th century by Louis I of Savoy; it now contains the **Military Museum of Vaud** (open Jul–Aug Tues–Sun 10am–5pm, Sept–Jun Tues–Fri 10am–noon, 1.30–5pm, Sat–Sun 1.30–5pm; admission fee), displaying uniforms, flags, arms and 8,000 tiny leaden soldiers. In the Grand-Rue, the museum inside the 16th-century **Alexis Forel house** has a collection of furniture, porcelain and glass, as well as antique dolls and toys.

Lausanne

There is always something happening in this prosperous city, capital of the canton of Vaud and headquarters of the International Olympic Committee (IOC). Cosmopolitan **Lausanne**'s attractions include ballet (the Béjart company), classical music concerts, operas, jazz, theatre, cinema (the Swiss *cinemathèque*) and fairs.

The history of *Lousonna* goes back to Roman times, when it was an important crossroads for trade. An episcopal city since the beginning of the 12th century, Lausanne grew in economic importance over the course of the Middle Ages. In 1537, the Academy (later to be a university) was created, giving this religious and commercial centre an intellectual bent. Since 1874, Lausanne has been the seat of the Federal Tribunal, the highest judicial body in the Swiss Confederation.

Ouchy, situated on the banks of Lake Geneva, is the liveliest part of town, with parks, cafés, a château (now a hotel) and the Olympic Museum *(see page 115)*. From the port, large white steamers leave for Vevey, Montreux, Evian, Thonon, Morges, Nyon and Geneva.

A stone's throw from Ouchy, and also located on the lake's edge, is the **Vidy Theatre**. This hosts productions (sometimes in their

Lausanne Cathedral

European premiere) by such well-known directors as Peter Brook and Robert Wilson.

To leave Ouchy for the **place Saint-François**, a commercial square built around a 13th-century church, take what the locals call the *métro* or the *ficelle* (meaning piece of string, basically a funicular between Ouchy and the old town). From Saint-François, you can follow the boutique-lined rue de Bourg to the rue Caroline, before crossing the Bessières bridge.

There is no need to describe the way to the **cathedral**; it is impossible to miss as it looms before you. Built in Burgundian Gothic style and finished in 1275, the cathedral retains some remarkable vestiges of the 13th century, including some lovely **choir stalls** and a **rose window** in the transept. An ancient tradition is still observed in the sanctuary: every night, between 10pm and 2am, a crier announces the hours to the city from the top of the church tower.

The old episcopal palace, located next door to the cathedral, currently holds the **Musée Historique de Lausanne** (Historical Museum of Lausanne; open Tues–Thur 11am–6pm, Fri–Sun 11am–5pm; also open Mon Jul–Aug; admission fee). Temporary exhibitions are also shown here.

Covered staircases descend from the cathedral to the **place de la Palud**, which has hosted an outdoor market since the Middle Ages (now held on Wednesday and Saturday mornings). This does not detract from the solemn dignity of Lausanne's 17th-century **Hôtel de Ville** (town hall), with its attractive ensemble of arches, clock tower and gargoyles.

The town has a dozen or so museums devoted to subjects ranging from the history of the Olympics to that of pipe-smokers. But the most original museum in Switzerland may be the **Collection of Primitive Art** (*Art Brut*; open Tues–Sun 11am–6pm; admission fee; <www.artbrut.ch>), which is housed in a 13th-century castle, near the palace of Beaulieu.

This dazzling collection of art by untrained artists, including psychiatric patients, was founded by the artist Jean Dubuffet.

North of Lausanne is the **Hermitage Foundation** (open Tues–Sun 10am–6pm, Thur until 9pm; admission fee), with a view of the lake and the historic town centre; temporary painting exhibitions are held here.

The **Musée de l'Elysée** (18 avenue de l'Elysée; open daily 11am–6pm; admission fee) occupies an appealing 19th-century residence. It specialises in photography, inviting visitors to trace the history of the art, from the daguerrotype to ultramodern techniques. It also offers a rich programme of frequently changing exhibitions.

The **Olympic Museum** (1 quai d'Ouchy; open Apr–Oct daily 9am–6pm, Nov–Mar Tues–Sun 9am–6pm; admission fee; <www.museum.olympic.org>) has a detailed display on the history of sports and the Olympic movement.

The sculpture *Ouverture au Monde* in Ouchy, by Angelo Duarte

The Vaud Riviera

This region extends from the suburbs of Lausanne to the eastern edge of Lake Geneva. Villette, Epesses and Saint-Saphorin are typical wine-growing villages, depicted in literature by C.F. Ramuz, a writer from the Vaud region. Whatever your method of transport (boat, train or car), the landscapes of the Lavaux are something to see.

Just before Vevey, at Corseaux, a white wall draws your eye: it is the **Villa Le Corbusier**, designed in the early 1920s by Le Corbusier and Pierre Jeanneret.

Chocolate and wine are the twin foundations of **Vevey**'s fortune. In fact, the largest building in town, a glass structure with concave walls, is the worldwide centre for Nestlé, the multinational food manufacturer. And viticulture, the region's other important resource, has given rise to the Fête des Vignerons (Vineyard Festival), celebrated every 25 years or so since the 16th century (the last one was in 1999). This popular festival brings together thousands of willing partici-

Chocolate and Cheese

Want to combine three of Switzerland's most famous activities (tasting cheese, sampling chocolate and taking a scenic train ride) into one adventure? The Chocolate Train takes travellers in either a Pullman car or panoramic train from Montreux to the popular cheese town of Gruyères and then on to the Nestlé-Cailler chocolate factory in Broc. At Gruyères, you will tour a cheese-making facility and taste its famous cheese. You will also be able to tour the castle. Then, you continue on to Broc, where the famous Swiss version of Nestlé chocolate is made. After a brief video and tour, the visit ends in the tasting room, filled with samples of each Cailler chocolate variety and complemented by tasting tips and tidbits on the different chocolates. For more information, go to <www.myswitzerland.raileurope.com>.

pants from the region, creating a splendid spectacle.

The old town is a wonderful place to explore. Among the 18th- and 19th-century houses are squares with many fine old fountains.

A cog train goes from Vevey to **Les Pleiades**, a belvedere with a panoramic vista at 1,360m (4,460ft) above sea level. Here you can take in the entire lake with the Alps behind it. Halfway up, **Blonay** is both the site of a 12th-century

Boats on the lake off Montreux

castle and the end of the line for a small tourist railway (the Blonay-Chamby line; <www.blonay-chamby.ch>) whose steam engine and cars date from the early 20th century.

Far above the vineyards and orchards of Vevey, a funicular climbs to the next vista, **Mont-Pèlerin**. Don't miss the panoramic tower, the 'Plein Ciel' (Open Sky), with a 360° view of the whole lake region.

Near the far end of the lake, the fin-de-siècle palaces of **Montreux** attract tourists all year round. Vladimir Nabokov, author of *Lolita*, spent his final days in one of these hotels. Montreux owes its Mediterranean atmosphere to a microclimate, which favours all kinds of blossoming plants. The town is also the setting for international shows such as the prestigious Montreux Jazz Festival (July; <www.montreuxjazz.com>), the Musical September classical music festival and the Festival of Laughter (December). The casino, Switzerland's first, looks out on the lakefront, adding to this resort's appeal.

The famous Château de Chillon

The **old town**, tucked into the hillside, also charms, with its 18th-century stone houses, antiques shops and artisans' boutiques.

A mountain train climbs to **Rochers-de-Naye** (<www.mob.ch>), at an elevation of more than 2,000m (6,560ft), passing through orchards, pastures and forests: the views along the way are stupendous. The site is also a haven for hikers, rock-climbers and skydivers.

If you like your landscapes as seen through a window, board the unique Panoramic Express. A brainchild of the Montreux-Oberland Bernois (MOB; <www.mob.ch>), this train offers unbeatable views over Lake Geneva before continuing on to Gruyères, Château-d'Oex, Rougemont, Gstaad, Zweisimmen, Interlaken and Lucerne.

 East of Montreux, the most celebrated of all Swiss châteaux, the **Château de Chillon** (open daily Apr–Sept 9am–6pm, Mar and Oct 9.30am–5pm, Nov–Feb 10am–4pm; admission fee; <www.chillon.ch>), is an austere feudal fortress, oddly wedged between the lake and the railway line. The great rock of Chillon, projecting out over Lake Geneva, was always a natural stronghold from which to guard the major Saint Bernard road linking Rome to its northern provinces. There were probably fortifications on the spot since ancient times, and a rudimentary château, which belonged to the bishops of Sion, was later fortified and enlarged by the dukes of Savoy. In 1536, after a three-day siege, the fortress fell into the hands of the Bernese.

Four Resorts in Vaud

The resorts of Vaud have developed modern infrastructures without losing their Old-World character. It is this balance that accounts for their popularity and appeal.

Château-d'Oex (960m/3,150ft; <www.chateau-doex.ch). A pleasant village snuggled into the welcoming valley of the Pays d'Enhaut, it is ideal for family vacations. The interesting Musée du Pays d'Enhaut showcases the arts, crafts and history of the region. You can also visit Etivaz to watch local craftsmen make the cheese of the same name. At the end of January, one of the most famous international airshows takes place here, bringing together over 100 hot-air balloons.

Les Diablerets (1,150m/3,770ft; <www.diablerets.ch>). This family-style resort occupies a beautiful Alpine site. A cable car makes three stops on the way to the top of one of Switzerland's most impressive glaciers – Les Diablerets (3,000m/9,840ft), where you can ski all year round, hike on the glacier, or go for a dog sled ride.

Leysin (1,250m/4,100ft; <www.leysin.ch>). This spectacular sunny spot, facing the Dents du Midi and the Mont Blanc mountain range, has beginning and intermediate-level ski slopes. Each January, Leysin plays host to the European Snowboard Championship.

Villars-sur-Ollon (1,250m/4,100ft; <www.villars.ch>). A family resort full of activity at weekends, with sports ranging from downhill and cross-country skiing and skating, to horseback riding, swimming, tennis and golf. Gryon (1,110m/3,640ft) is a continuation of and complement to Villars. Gryon has preserved its traditional character, and its abundant fauna and flora make it an unmissable gem.

FRIBOURG, NEUCHÂTEL AND THE JURA

These three neighbouring cantons have very distinct characters and strong personalities of their own.

Fribourg

The hilly terrain of **Fribourg** has made it a town in three dimensions, built at once along the Sarine river (*Saane* in German) and on a cliff above it. What first strikes the visitor's eye is the harmony between the wild gorges and the marvellous Gothic buildings.

Founded in 1157 by Duke Berchtold IV of Zähringen, Fribourg joined the Confederation in 1481. When the Reformation seized Bern, Fribourg resisted. Today, it remains steadfastly Catholic, with its churches, seminaries and theological bookshops. Fribourg is also a bilingual town.

Historic Fribourg, on the Sarine river

Zähringen Bridge offers the classic view of the river, the 13th-
and 15th-century ramparts on the steep hillside, and the old
covered bridge linking the banks of the Sarine. There has
been a bridge at this point since the 13th century.

Like most historical buildings in Fribourg, the **Cathédrale
Saint-Nicolas** is made of sandstone. Age, weather and pol-
lution have left their mark. The Gothic statues that frame the
main portal are copies; the originals are in the Catholic University and the Museum of Art and History. Inside the cathedral, note the striking sculptural ensemble *Entombment of
Christ* (1433) in the Chapel of the Holy Sepulchre.

Another important architectural work is the **Eglise de
Cordeliers**, founded in the 13th century by Franciscan monks.
Among its highlights are the oak choir stalls (1280), a fine
altarpiece (1480) above the main altar and, in one of the side
chapels, a triptych of sculpted and gilded wood (1513).

The **Musée d'Art et d'Histoire** (Art and History Museum; open Tues–Sun 11am–6pm, Thur until 8pm; admission
fee) is installed in the Hôtel Ratzé, a splendid Renaissance
residence; part of it also occupies a nearby 19th-century
slaughterhouse. The eclectic collections of this museum are
based on the past of Fribourg and its immediate environs.

Next to the Art and History Museum, the space devoted
to the works of Fribourg native Jean Tinguely and his com-
panion Nicki de Saint-Phalle is a definite must (open Wed–
Sun 11am–6pm, Thur until 8pm; admission fee).

The **Hôtel de Ville** (town hall), notable for its great sloping roof, its covered ceremonial staircase and turreted clock
tower, dates from the early 16th century.

Around Fribourg

Murten (Morat). This bilingual town is a marvel of perfectly preserved old houses with deep arcades and overhanging
roofs. You can climb up to the medieval towers and ramparts

to survey the tile roofs, the town's little lake and the countryside. Also worthy of note here is the 13th-century castle and the solid Bern Gate, with its bell and belfry. In summer, some excursion boats go from the Murten lake to Biel and Neuchâtel.

Avenches. *Aventicum* was the capital of Roman Helvetia. Around AD260, it was sacked by Alemanni tribesmen, and no one knows what happened to its 20,000 inhabitants. In the Middle Ages a new town was founded on the same site, but its prosperity never approached that of the ancient capital.

At the far end of the rue Centrale, visit the **amphitheatre**, where 8,000 spectators could gather to watch gladiators in the Roman era. Today, it is used for open-air operas. Above the main entrance, a medieval tower now houses the **Roman Museum** (open Tues–Sun Apr–Sept 10am–noon, 1–5pm, Oct–Mar 2–5pm; admission fee), whose well-presented collections are supplied by ongoing archaeological digs. Around Avenches there are several other Roman ruins to visit, including a theatre and parts of the ancient wall.

Payerne. This small town in the Broye valley is home to the **Abbatiale**, the largest Romanesque church in the country and the only remaining vestige of an important Benedictine abbey. After the Reformation, this remarkable building was abandoned. But more than a half-century of restorations have revealed architectural elements from the 11th century, such as the majestic columns supporting the vaulted ceiling.

Gruyères. This large, fortified medieval village, high on a hilltop, draws tourists from the world over. Arrive early in summer. The **castle** (open daily Apr–Oct 9am–6pm, Nov–Mar 10am–4.30pm; admission fee), built by the counts of Gruyères in the 12th century, is definitely worth a visit, if only for the view from the battlements. The worn steps of the spiral staircase lead you to the well-preserved state rooms and private apartments.

Don't leave Gruyères without tasting some of its specialities: fondue and meringue, raspberries and blueberries, all served with the thick, smooth cream particular to this region. At the foot of the hill, a model dairy shows you the secrets involved in making the famous Gruyère cheese (open daily Jun–Sept 9am–7pm, Oct–May 9am–6pm; admission fee; <www.lamaisondugruyere.ch>).

Bulle, 11km (7 miles) from Gruyères, is the site of a fine 13th-century castle (not open to visitors) and the **Gruyères Museum**, which illustrates the customs of the region.

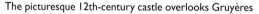

The picturesque 12th-century castle overlooks Gruyères

Neuchâtel

The lakeside town of **Neuchâtel** has a long intellectual tradition, which lives on in its university, its schools and its specialised institutes. The town has belonged successively to the Holy Roman Empire, the dukes of Burgundy and the kings of Prussia. It was not until 1857 that Prussia officially recognised the independence of the canton, even though it had been a Confederation member since 1815. The 'tick-tock' of official Swiss time is emitted by the Chronometric Observatory of Neuchâtel, the research centre for the clockmaking industry.

The old crossroads of the Croix du Marché, a few streets in from the port, contains buildings and fountains constructed between the 16th and 18th centuries. The most original structure in this area is the **Maison des Halles** (1575), which was once a covered market.

Neuchâtel's Collégiale

The town is dominated by a monumental group of medieval buildings, where once church, prison and government shared a fortified enclosure. Inside the **Collégiale** (collegiate church), a remarkable sculpture immortalises the counts of Neuchâtel. The castle (12th–16th centuries) is now the seat of the cantonal government. The top of the prison tower (15th century) commands the best view of the town and the lake. To the west, on rue

Saint-Nicolas, the **Musée d'Ethnographie** (Ethnographic Museum; open Tues–Sun 10am–5pm; admission fee) has several good collections relating to Ancient Egypt, Africa and Oceania. The **Musée d'Art et d'Histoire**, on Esplanade Léopold-Robert close to the port, is dedicated to Swiss artists and to religious paintings of the Middle Ages. It brings together rare Swiss ceramics, 16th-century watches, armour, coins and medallions (open Tues–Sun 11am–6pm; admission fee).

Around Neuchâtel Lake

The charming town of **Grandson** was the scene of a famous triumph in Swiss history: the 1476 defeat of Charles the Bold, Duke of Burgundy, by Confederate troops. At the castle, you can see a re-enactment of this event with lead soldiers. Climb the ramparts (13th century) to visit the museum of antique cars, featuring Greta Garbo's 1923 Rolls-Royce.

Yverdon-les-Bains, known for its mineral baths since Roman times, is once again flourishing as a spa. In the centre of town, a 13th-century castle houses the municipal museum. One room is devoted to Pestalozzi, a pioneer of pedagogy, who ran a school here in the 19th century.

Many varied architectural styles coexist in the walled town of **Estavayer-le-Lac**, on the south bank of Neuchâtel Lake. The Château de Chenaux dates from the 13th century, while the Saint-Laurent church in the heart of town is mainly of late Gothic style. A most surprising attraction is the **Museum of Frogs** (open Jul–Aug daily 10am–noon, 2–5pm; Mar–Jun and Sept–Oct Tues–Sun 10am–noon, 2–5pm; Nov–Feb Sat–Sun 2–5pm; <www.museedesgrenouilles.ch>), filled with over 100 stuffed frogs in surreal poses.

The Jura

French-speaking **Jura**, established in 1979, is the baby among Swiss cantons. The Jurassic range links Geneva to Basel, accompanying the French border on one side and stretching across half a dozen Swiss cantons on the other. It is a zone of meadows, lakes and fir forests interspersed with the region's typical dwellings, enclosed in dry-stone walls. Life is harsh in this sparsely populated region, where for centuries watchmaking, practised at home, was the economic mainstay. Switzerland appears less opulent and prosperous here. But for the tourist seeking peace and beauty, the Jura is a great discovery.

The magnificent village of **Romainmôtier**, tucked into an idyllic valley, takes its name from the monastery (*moûtier* in old French) founded here around AD450 by Saint Romain. The church, dating from the 10th and 11th centuries, is absolutely remarkable. You can still see, on the floor in front of the organ, the traces of two earlier churches. The frescoes are from the 12th and 13th centuries; the Romanesque sculptures represent demons and wonders of the medieval world. In the choir, there is a sculpted 7th-century ambon (an early kind of pulpit). The 14th-century clock tower and the 15th-century priory are all that remains of the monastery.

Early Le Corbusier

Native son Le Corbusier realised some of his first architectural projects in La Chaux-de-Fonds. The fruits of this era include the Fallet villa (1906, decorated in Jurassian Art Nouveau), the Jacquemet villa (1908) and the Stotzer villa (1908). The architect's character can be clearly seen in the mature design of the Villa Turque (1917). Some time after these projects were completed, Le Corbusier moved to Paris.

The main attraction of **La Chaux-de-Fonds**, a town of 40,000 inhabitants devoted to clockmaking, is the 'Man and Time' exhibition at the **Musée International d'Horlogerie** (International Clockmaking Museum; open Tues–Sun 10am–5pm; admission fee; <www.mih.ch>). It is unique, both architecturally – the museum is entirely underground – and

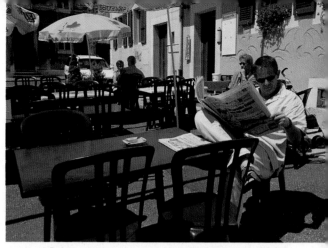

Relaxing in the mountain town of La Chaux-de-Fonds

in its collection. With over 3,000 timepieces on display, from sundials to hourglasses to chronometers of the most modern kind, it is the most important museum of its kind in the world. Note especially the 17th-century enamelled watches.

To the north of the town begin the forests and pastures of the **Franches-Montagnes**. This peaceful region's main activity is the raising of horses. **Saignelégier**, the county seat, welcomes important events each year, such as the Horse Fair and Market (in summer) and the dogsled races (in winter).

The impetuous Doubs river, originating in France, encloses the delightful little town of **Saint-Ursanne**, where pink, white and ochre-coloured stone houses vie for space on the riverbank. After crossing the narrow, swaybacked bridge, you enter the walled town, where life revolves around the **Collégiale** (collegiate church). Like the village, the church takes its name from Saint Ursinicus, an Irish pilgrim of the 12th century, who lived as a hermit in the Doubs valley.

WHAT TO DO

SPORTS

Downhill skiing. Whether you're a champion or a beginner, Switzerland remains the homeland of this sport, offering the best possible conditions of comfort and safety, not to mention the most beautiful landscapes.

Nearly 200 villages and towns are equipped for downhill skiing: Valais offers a wide choice of resorts, including Zermatt, Crans-Montana, Saas-Fee or Champéry, from which you can reach the Portes du Soleil (650km/400 miles of slopes, with 230 mechanical lifts). The Grisons range also has superb skiing, with St Moritz, Pontresina, Davos and Klosters, as well as Flims and Laax, with their Alpenarena. The Alps of Vaud, the Jura and central Switzerland also offer wonderful ski slopes.

In most regions the season lasts from late November through to early April, but conditions vary according to the year and the resort. The high seasons (when prices and crowds are at their height) are Christmas, Easter and February. Outside of these times, you can get better package deals. Throughout winter, Swiss ski schools organise group courses taught by qualified instructors, who will also give private lessons.

Before hitting the slopes, don't forget to bring sunblock and sunglasses to protect you from the blinding glare. Be cautious: regulate your speed according to your physical condition and level of expertise in order to avoid having to call the security patrols (efficient and well-equipped though they are).

Snowboarding. Snowboarders will not be disappointed with what Switzerland has to offer. Besides the slopes that can be shared with skiers, many resorts are setting aside areas with jumps, obstacle courses and a young, 'cool' atmosphere (Grindelwald First and Adelboden Hahnenmoos, to name two).

Snowblading. This recent addition to the world of winter sports, practised on shorter skis without poles, is wonderfully exhilarating. If you don't dare go it alone at first, many ski schools offer snowblading courses.

Cross-country skiing (*Langlauf* in German). This sport has come back into fashion in recent years. Glide through the wooded countryside or follow a stream or river, stopping along the way for a picnic or lunch on a restaurant terrace. The tracks are groomed and ranked according to difficulty. Some resorts have up to 100km (60 miles) of tracks, and new ones are being opened each year. The Jura, Engadine and Appenzell are particularly popular locations.

Skating. Most resorts have natural or artificial rinks open throughout the winter. Skate hire and lessons are available.

Curling. This sport, which involves sliding heavy polished blocks of stone across a rectangular track of ice, can be practised in many places in Switzerland. Both open-air and covered tracks are available.

Sled Runs

For a thrill of a lifetime, consider three downhill sled runs in the St Moritz area. At the Cresta Run, the rider hurtles headfirst down an ice track on a skeleton sled at speeds of up to 140kph (87mph). Those who would prefer to leave the driving to a professional, might consider the St Moritz/Celerina Olympia Bobrun. Here, riders race on a real bobsled course with a professional driver in front and brakeman at the back. Visit the St Moritz tourist website at <www.stmoritz.ch> or call 081 837 3333 for more information on these two runs.

For a slower descent, consider the Preda-Bergun toboggan run just outside St Moritz in Bergun. On this track, riders travel at their leisure on wooden sleds for a fraction of the cost. Contact the Bergun tourist office at 081 407 1152 for more information.

Skydiving and hang-gliding. The Swiss terrain is very well suited to these adventure sports (at Lenzerheide, Rigi, Salève and St Moritz).

Summer skiing. In resorts near glaciers, such as Les Diablerets, Verbier, Zermatt, Saas-Fee and Pontresina, you can easily ski all morning and swim all afternoon. Many of them operate lifts and cable cars all summer.

Rock-climbing. A professional guide and adequate equipment are of crucial importance for this sport. Rescuers often bewail the carelessness of people who dress as if for a tennis match

Cross-country skiing, Engadine

to make their way over difficult, often unpredictable rockfaces. The best option for newcomers is to take a climbing course.

Mountain trekking. Trekking is less dangerous than climbing, but it is still important to take precautions and to be well equipped, with good shoes and the right clothing. Be careful not to leave the marked paths. For greater safety, get detailed maps from the local tourist office. The Swiss Alpine Club also has a list of huts available in the mountains.

Hiking. Switzerland has about 50,000km (31,250 miles) of marked hiking trails. Wherever you go, you will see yellow signs that designate the trails and indicate the journey time to the next checkpoint. It is easy to find books, leaflets or maps suggesting the most attractive hiking destinations in the region.

Swimming. Switzerland's lakefronts, beaches and creeks are available to everyone. Most cities and resorts have beaches as well as swimming pools, not to mention the thermal baths at resorts such as Bad Ragaz, Leukerbad, Yverdon, Ovronnaz and Scuol.

Windsurfing. You can hire equipment to experience this ever-more-popular sport; instructors will help you get yourself up and afloat.

Waterskiing. This expensive sport is practised at most major resorts, although on some lakes it is forbidden for environmental reasons.

Sailing. Hardly a weekend goes by in summer without a major regatta taking place somewhere in Switzerland. You can hire yachts or paddleboats on most lakes. You will need a permit to navigate a sailboat with a sail larger than 14 sq m (46 sq ft), but you can content yourself with a small dinghy

Hikers near the Ofen Pass in the Swiss National Park, Grisons or a canoe. Beware the sudden gusts of wind that often arise on the lakes.

Fishing. Lakes and rivers are restocked every year (with trout, char and pike). The local police station issues permits for a day, week or year, and will notify you of the regulations, which vary from one spot to the next.

Golf. There are about 30 courses throughout Switzerland. In the Alps, every possibility for building a golf course seems to have been explored (in St Moritz, you can play golf all winter on a frozen lake). If you belong to a golf club in your own country, you will usually be admitted to one here for a small fee.

Swiss wrestling

Folklore and sport meet in the ancient tradition of Swiss wrestling (*Hosenlupf*). The wrestlers, wearing special leggings, clash grimly until one of them throws his adversary into the sawdust, all according to the strictest rules. There is fighting of a very different kind in the Valais region: 'combats of the queens' (cow fights) attract crowds every Sunday in spring.

Tennis. Many of the resorts and most big cities have tennis courts, although the city facilities are often overrun with people. Lessons are available. Every summer, the Swiss Open, the Gstaad International Championship, attracts the world's best players.

Horse riding. There are stables and riding schools on the outskirts of major cities, as well as in vacation spots. Contact the Swiss tourist office *(see page 171)* or ask a travel agent about the particulars of an equestrian vacation.

Cycling and mountain biking. You can hire a bike at a railway station and take it back to any other station when you get tired. Switzerland's terrain makes it an ideal place for mountain biking. Ask at the local tourist office for recommended routes; detailed maps are available as well. Remember, though: you'll need strong calves and good lungs.

SHOPPING

Cheeses, chocolate and cuckoo clocks: these are the first items that shopping in Switzerland brings to mind, but there are many other possibilities. Luxury goods, such as furs, watches and jewels, are the best deals available. On the other hand, many everyday articles may seem expensive here, due to the strength of the Swiss franc. But the quality of the items is rarely in question, as the Swiss themselves are demanding consumers. Salespeople are generally courteous and efficient.

Look out for good buys during the annual sale periods of January–February and July–August. No taxes need be added: the price on the label is the price you pay.

Where to Shop

Zurich and Geneva are known all over the world for their chic boutiques, as are Basel and Bern and resorts such as Gstaad and St Moritz. If your budget doesn't allow you the occasional splurge, you can find reasonable buys in department stores, where prices seldom vary from one canton to the next.

What to Buy

Liquor. Fruit brandies *(eaux-de-vie)* are easy to transport and make excellent souvenirs or gifts: they include apple, kirsch (cherry), marc (made from champagne), pear, plum and gentian.

Antiques. Whatever you're looking for, you can find it here. Luxury antiques shops and secondhand dealers are everywhere. To find silver and old jewellery or any other precious object, go to the auctions held in Zurich or Geneva. And don't turn up your nose at street fairs and flea markets, where it's always possible to discover a real find.

Art. Art galleries abound, in small towns and big cities alike. Specialists in the field make sure that Swiss prices remain

A well-known brand: the Swiss Army Knife by Victorinox

competitive with foreign ones, and merchants are glad to ship paintings and sculptures anywhere in the world.

Cheese. Merchants can tell you which cheeses will survive the trip home and will wrap them accordingly *(see page 140)*.

Chocolate. Switzerland produces what is easily the largest variety of chocolates in the world. Milk chocolate, particularly, is of the highest quality. You will find an amazing choice of truffles in luxury chocolate shops.

Embroidery. St-Gallen has made its reputation in the world of embroidery; look especially for napkins, tablecloths, blouses and handkerchiefs.

Jewellery. Jewels and gold are of the highest quality here. Gaze at the sumptuous window displays on major shopping streets, but don't neglect tiny stores in side streets of old towns.

Knives. The Swiss Army Knife – a little tool kit that fits in your pocket – can include more than 30 features, from a corkscrew to a miniature saw. It can take on any task.

Watches and clocks. From the 'disposable' watch to the finest timepiece, the choice here is immense. You can rest assured that whatever model you choose will come with an international guarantee. If you want something fancier than a Swatch, choose a Rolex, an Audemars Piguet or a Blancpain.

As for cuckoo clocks, they do really exist, in every size, in department stores and souvenir boutiques. If the little bird who chirps the hours isn't serious enough for you, perhaps a pendulum clock from Neuchâtel will tempt you instead.

Souvenirs. Some local choices include cowbells, collectable dolls and yodelling records, but there are also fossils or rocks from the Alps, crafted objects from the *Heimatwerk* (home-craft) boutiques, wooden toys, bowls, plates, music boxes, copper, pewter, painted Easter eggs and landscapes or silhouettes cut out of paper.

ENTERTAINMENT

Swiss cities have a livelier nightlife than you might imagine. Even in relatively isolated places, it is not unusual to find a disco, an outdoor dance or a concert. But in a country where work often begins at 7am, night crawlers are a rare sight.

Traditional music

During festivals, or in market places, you will often hear the sombre sound of the alphorn, a curious wind instrument of astonishing size. Another unique Swiss sound, yodelling, may be encountered in restaurants in German-speaking areas, as well as at festivals.

Nightclubs that offer floor shows and orchestras exist only in the bigger cities. Elsewhere, entertainment is often limited to a piano player, but there is a certain charm in the simpler pleasures Switzerland has to offer, like sharing a good bottle of wine by a fire in a mountain chalet, or taking a 'dancing cruise' on a lake.

International tours by important musical artists invariably include a few Swiss cities among their stops. Swiss chamber orchestras and symphonies, such as the famous Orchestre de la Suisse Romande, often give concerts. Look into the possibility of hearing medieval music in a castle courtyard, or an organ recital in an old church. There are also frequent music festivals in the area, the most famous of which is held in Lucerne in August.

Opera and dance performances are easy to find in Zurich, Geneva, Basel, Bern, Lausanne and St-Gallen.

Jazz, both traditional and avant-garde, is not neglected either, but all the concerts to be heard around the country during the year are just warm-ups for the Montreux Festival.

Swiss theatre is well regarded everywhere; good local troupes alternate with foreign companies on tour. Every genre is represented, and the productions are of the highest quality.

Curtain call: the elaborate Chamber Theatre in Bern

CHILDREN'S SWITZERLAND

Tobogganing is a favourite activity for children of all ages and can be found in most mountain resorts. Some areas have illuminated pistes for night runs, such as at Grindelwald in the Bernese Oberland. Many resorts also have skating rinks. In the warmer months, children will enjoy the hiking and biking trails, as well as play areas.

Switzerland's many lakes provide a multitude of fun activities during the spring and summer, including boat rides and hiring a paddle boat. Most cities have public swimming beaches, some with water slides, as in Geneva. Also, near Montreux, there is a large water park in Le Bouveret.

There are festivals all year round, and most will have activities for children. Some of the larger festivals have rides and games, including the *Fêtes de Genève* in August. Basel's *Fasnacht* is one of the most famous festivals in the country.

Switzerland has two of the best zoos in Europe at Basel and Zurich (<www.zoo.ch>). Basel's, the largest in the country, is particularly known for the successful breeding of endangered species *(see page 40)*.

A cowbell at the cattle festival in Urnäsch

There are also a number of museums that will interest children, including the Jean Tinguely Museum in Basel *(see page 42)* with its machines and gadgets, the Verkehrshaus transport museum in Lucerne *(see page 68)* with its aeroplanes and locomotives, and the Swissminiatur museum near Lugano *(see page 91)* with its miniature models of all things Swiss.

Calendar of Events

Quite apart from the international cultural festivals in the major cities, there is no Swiss village, no matter how small, that does not put on at least one festival a year. Regional tourist offices publish annual brochures listing all the celebrations planned for the region.

January. Celebrations ring in the New Year. Horse races in the snow in St Moritz and Arosa; Vogel-Gryff Day in Basel; *Silvesterklausen* in Urnäsch, where men dress up in traditional masked costumes.

February/March. Carnival *(Fasnacht)* in Bern, Basel, Lucerne and other Catholic parts of Switzerland.

March. In Engadine, the *Chalanda März* (a children's procession of pagan origin) and the ski marathon with thousands of participants.

April. *Sechseläuten* in Zurich: bonfires with Old Man Winter, known locally as the *Böogg*; parades. Procession of weeping women in Romont.

April/May. *Landsgemeinde* in Appenzell; 'combats of the queens' (cow fights) that attract crowds every Sunday in Valais. Open House at wineries in the Geneva area.

June. Herding of cows up the Alps. International Festival in Zurich (three weeks of concerts, opera, theatre and exhibitions).

July. Jazz festival in Montreux and Paléo music festival in Nyon. East Switzerland Yodellers' Festival in Chur. Opera Festival in the amphitheatre of Avenches. 'Estival Jazz' in Lugano.

August. National Day (1 Aug). Music festivals in Lucerne and Gstaad. International film festival in Locarno. Fireworks and parades at the *Fêtes de Genève* (Geneva). Street Parade (techno music festival) in Zurich.

September. Music festivals in Montreux and Vevey. Swiss crafts fair in Lausanne. *Désalpe*, descent of the cows in Charmey (near Gruyères).

September/October. Wine harvest *(vendange* in French) festivals in Geneva, Lugano and Neuchâtel.

November. Onion market *(Zibelemärit)* in Bern (fourth Monday). Autumn fair in Basel.

December. The *Escalade* historical procession in Geneva.

EATING OUT

The Swiss like to eat and drink well and they offer their visitors enough choices to satisfy any taste, from the popular fare served in village bistros to the refined gourmet menus of world-class restaurants. Each region has its own specialities, often influenced by the traditions of the neighbouring country whose language is spoken there.

Meaty fondues

Those who like meat and cheese together might try a *fondue bourguignonne* (Burgundian fondue) or *chinoise* (Chinese fondue).

Fondues and Cheeses

A fondue is more than a meal, it's a party. Guests gather around a *caquelon* (cast-iron dish) bubbling with cheese melted with white wine (and a shot of kirsch) and, armed with long fondue forks, dip in their hunks of country bread. Besides the familiar Gruyère fondue, there are creamier variants, such as the *moitié-moitié* (half-and-half), where the Gruyère is mixed with Vacherin cheese from Fribourg, or the Fribourg fondue, which is made from Vacherin alone. There are also fondues containing wild mushrooms or tomatoes.

Raclette is a cousin of fondue. A half-wheel of cheese is placed in front of a heat source – traditionally a hearth – and when the cheese begins to melt, a portion is scraped off. The cheese falls onto your plate next to a boiled potato, onions cured in vinegar and *cornichons* (tiny pickled gherkins).

Only white wine or hot tea should be drunk with fondue or *raclette*; cold drinks are said to inhibit digestion. The same is true for the delicious pastries called *malakoffs*, a kind of savoury doughnut made with Gruyère.

Cheeses. These do not make up a course in themselves, as in France, but are served as *hors-d'oeuvre*s or at late-night suppers, accompanied by baked potatoes. Emmental is a sweet cheese full of holes. Appenzell is a sharper version. The firm interior of Gruyère (*Greyerzer* in German) has only a few small holes and tastes of hazelnut. Gruyère exists in sweet, semi-salty and salty varieties. Sbrinz, a hard cheese, is served in *rebibes* (slices as thin as cigarette paper). Firm, round and strong-smelling *Tête-de-moine* (monk's head) is a Jura speciality. It is carved out, *raclette*-style, until it resembles a sort of fragrant mushroom. It is generally eaten in winter.

Tomme, a sweet, soft cheese from Vaud, is sometimes combined with cumin. Reblochon, a creamy cheese, is somewhat stronger. Finally, we should mention Schabziger, a herbed cheese from the canton of Glarus that smells pretty powerful.

For unexpected hunger pangs, take along a *ramequin* (*Chäschüechli* in German), a small cheese pie, or perhaps some cheese toast *(Käseschnite)*.

A sociable dish: sharing a fondue in Fribourg

Specialities of French Switzerland

Fish. The *omble chevalier*, or knight's char, the most delicate and delicious of freshwater fish, is usually poached and served with Hollandaise sauce or melted butter. Trout and its pink-fleshed cousin salmon trout are both excellent. Perch is most often served filleted and fried, with tartar sauce and a slice of lemon. Pike is either grilled or prepared in *quenelles* (dumplings), while *fera* fillets are baked or fried.

Meat. French influence is obvious in the *entrecôtes* (rib steaks) and *filet mignons* served here. *Assiette valaisienne* (Valais assortment) is made up of fine rolled slices of dried meat and bacon, smoked ham, sausage, cheese and tiny pickles. Wonderful with rye bread and a *déci* (or two) of Swiss white wine.

Rustic fare in Ticino

Specialities of Italian Switzerland

Piccata, pasta and pizza. In Ticino, you eat like an Italian. But *risotto* here is enhanced with onions, mushrooms and grated cheese.

Polenta, a thick corn purée, is served as an accompaniment to meat. Enriched with cream Ticino-style, it is called *polenta grassa* and restaurants stock this delicious mixture by the tureen. Taste these treats in a *grotto* – these establishments can be found in the most picturesque and romantic places.

Specialities of German Switzerland

Soups. *Basler Mehlsuppe* (grilled flour soup from Basel) is eaten early in the morning during Carnival season. Another favourite is *Brotsuppe* (bread soup from Lucerne).

Fish. One of the best is *fera (Felchen)*, fished from the region's many lakes. Perch *(Egli)* and trout *(Forelle)* are often raised in tanks. *Rötel*, from the Zug lake and *Äsche*, a cousin of the trout, are eaten only in late autumn and early winter.

Meat. *Geschnitzeltes Kalbfleisch* (sliced veal in cream sauce) is called *Emincé Zurichoise* in French-Swiss. *Berner Platte* (Bern assortment) consists of beef, sausages, sauerkraut or green beans and potatoes. *Bündnerfleisch* or Grison-style meat, is raw, air-dried beef eaten in paper-thin slices at the beginning of a meal.

Game. Game is popular from September to February, the hunting season. Roebuck *(Rehrücken)* is served with chestnuts, cranberry sauce and red cabbage. Other wild game dishes include deer *(hirsch)*, boar *(Wildschwein)* and hare *(Hase)*.

Sausages. There are at least 45 varieties of sausage, eaten boiled, fried, grilled, cold, smoked and even in salads. *Schüblig* is a pork sausage and *Bratwurst mit Zwiebelsauce* is veal sausage served with an onion sauce.

Side dishes. Don't leave this region without trying the *Rösti*, or grated, grilled potatoes. *Spätzli*, boiled pasta dumplings, are served with meat and game.

Desserts. Fruit pies are eaten for dessert or as snacks. No one can resist the *Zuger Kirschtorte*, the kirsch tart from Zug, or the *Rüeblitorte*, a cake made from carrots and eggs and topped with almonds, cinnamon and fruit brandy. Finally, the wonderful walnut pie is a speciality of Engadine.

Along with the tiny fruits that grow so well in the mountains – blueberries and raspberries, served with the rich *crème fraîche* of the Gruyère region – there are always delicious meringue desserts, served with or without whipped cream.

Swiss Wines

The reputation of Swiss wines has been steadily improving in recent years. The great wine-growing regions of Switzerland are the cantons of Valais, Vaud and Geneva. In bars and restaurants, wine can be ordered by the bottle or half-bottle, or in carafes of one or more decilitres. White wines are often remarkable here, derived mainly from the Chasselas grape, but also often from the Sylvaner (known as Johannisberg in Valais), which makes for a sweet bouquet. The best-known and most common wine is the fruity fendant, but you can also find Riesling, Pinot Gris or Pinot Blanc, Chardonnay or Dézaley, which is dry and very drinkable. Be sure to try Valais specialities such as Humagne Blanc, Petite Arvine and Amigne.

Fruit of the Vine

While touring the Lake Geneva area, be sure to visit two outstanding wine regions. First is the Lavaux, situated roughly between Montreux and Lausanne. The Lavaux is not only picturesque, with steep terraces rising off the banks of the lake, but it also produces some of Switzerland's finest white wines, with notable varietals including Chasselas and Pinot Blanc. You can hike or bike along the viticulture roads while taking in views of the vineyards and the French Alps across Lake Geneva. For a tasting, give Domaine Louis Bovard in Cully a try (tel: 021 799 2125). The other region not to miss is located in the countryside surrounding the city of Geneva. The Route du Vignoble wine road meanders through the rolling vineyards from the charming village of Satigny to the hilly region of Dardagny close to the French border. A few producers to try: Cave Les Perrières in Peissy (tel: 022 753 9000; <www.lesperrieres.ch>), Domaine du Paradis in Satigny (tel: 022 753 1855; <www.domaine-du-paradis.ch>) and Domaine Les Hutins in Dardagny (tel: 022 754 1205). Most wineries are open Saturday mornings for visitors.

Red wines are mainly of the Gamay and Pinot Noir varieties. In Ticino, the most prevalent wine is the robust Merlot, a strong red with a lovely ruby colour. Also, try Nostrano, a heady red wine, or Mezzana, which comes in both red and white. The German-Swiss wines are less widely known, but some of their light dry reds (Hallauer, Maienfelder, Klevner and Stammheimer) are well worth tasting.

Vines in La Côte, Vaud

Other Drinks

Swiss blonde beers are sold under many names, both bottled and draft. Like German beers, they tend to range in strength from medium to very strong. If you don't drink alcohol, try the local fruit juices, especially apple and grape.

Fruit brandy *(eau-de-vie)* is a common after-dinner drink. Among these liquors, which are very popular in Switzerland, try apple, prune, kirsch (in Basel and Zug), the *grappa* of Ticino, the *poire William* of Valais, or *chrüter*, a herbal brandy.

Coffee

At breakfast time, the customary drink is *Milchkaffee*, coffee with hot milk (called a *renversé* in French-speaking regions). The coffee here is generally less strong than that served in France or Italy. For an Italian-style espresso, ask for a *ristretto*. Coffee is always served with a small pot of cream; if you are lucky, the dish it comes in will be made of chocolate and filled with thick *crème fraîche*.

To Help you Order…
(…in three languages)
Waiter/Waitress
Garçon/Mademoiselle *Garçon/Fräulein* **Cameriere**

Can we have a table, please?
Une table,   *Wir hätten gern*   **Possiamo avere**
  s'il vous plaît.   *einen Tisch.*   **un tavolo?**

The menu, please.
La carte, s'il vous *Die Speisekarte,*   **Il menu,**
  plaît.   *bitte.*   **per favore.**

Do you have a special today?
Avez-vous une   *Haben Sie einen*   **Ha il piatto del**
  assiette du jour?   *Tagesteller?*   **giorno?**

I would like…
Je voudrais…   *Ich möchte…*   **Vorrei…**

a pre-dinner drink
un apéritif   *einen Aperitif*   **un aperitivo**

a beer	une bière	*einen Bier*	**una birra**
butter	du beurre	*Butter*	**del burro**
a coffee	un café	*einen Kaffee*	**un caffè**
water	de l'eau	*Wasser*	**dell'acqua**
cheese	du fromage	*Käse*	**del formaggio**
milk	du lait	*Milch*	**del latte**
bread	du pain	*Brot*	**del pane**
fish	du poisson	*Fisch*	**del pesce**
potatoes	des pommes de terre	*Kartoffeln*	**delle patate**
salad	de la salade	*Salat*	**dell'insalata**

The Kornhauskeller in Bern, a restaurant in an old corn cellar

salt	du sel	*Salz*	*del sale*
sugar	du sucre	*Zucker*	*dello zucchero*
tea	un thé	*einen Tee*	*un té*
wine	du vin	*Wein*	*del vino*

Reading the menu in French…

agneau	**lamb**	lard	**bacon**
asperges	**asparagus**	macédoine de fruits	**fruit salad**
bœuf	**beef**	médallion	**tenderloin**
canard	**duck**		
champignons	**mushrooms**	œufs	**eggs**
chasse	**game**	pomme	**apple**
chevreuil	**venison**	porc	**pork**
côte(lette)	**chop, cutlet**	poulet	**chicken**
entrecôte	**steak**	raisins	**grapes**
fraises	**strawberries**	saucisse	**sausage**

gigot (d'agneau)	**leg of lamb**	saumon (fumé)	**salmon (smoked)**
glace	**ice-cream**	terrine	**paté**
jambon	**ham**	veau	**veal**

and in German...

Apfel	**apple**	*Käse*	**cheese**
Bohnen	**beans**	*Kuchen*	**cake**
Ei(er)	**egg(s)**	*Lammfleisch*	**lamb**
Eis (Glace)	**ice**	*Leber*	**liver**
Ente	**duck**	*Rahm*	**cream**
Erbsen	**peas**	*Reis*	**rice**
Erdbeeren	**strawberries**	*Rindfleisch*	**beef**
Forelle	**trout**	*Rösti*	**potatoes**
Fruchtsalat	**fruit salad**	*Schinken*	**ham**
Geflügel	**poultry**	*Schweinefleisch*	**pork**
Gemüse	**grilled sliced vegetables**	*Spargel*	**asparagus**
		Speck	**bacon**
grüne Bohnen	**green beans**	*Teigwaren*	**noodles**
Huhn	**chicken**	*Wienerli*	**Vienna sausage**
Kalbfleisch	**veal**	*Wurst*	**sausage**

and in Italian...

agnello	**lamb**	*manzo*	**beef**
fagioli	**beans**	*polenta*	**polenta**
fagiolini	**green beans**	*pollo*	**chicken**
filetto	**filet (of beef)**	*prosciutto*	**ham**
formaggio	**cheese**	*riso*	**rice**
fragole	**strawberries**	*spinaci*	**spinach**
frutta	**fruit**	*trota*	**trout**
funghi	**mushrooms**	*uovo(a)*	**egg(s)**
gelato	**ice-cream**	*verdura*	**vegetables**
insalata	**salad**	*vitello*	**veal**

HANDY TRAVEL TIPS

An A–Z Summary of Practical Information

A

ACCOMMODATION (see also CAMPING and YOUTH HOSTELS)

Hotels of all categories are listed in the *Swiss Hotel Guide*, published annually by the Swiss Hotel Association (Monbijoustrasse 130, 3007 Bern, tel: 031 370 4111, <www.swisshotels.ch>). This association also provides leaflets with information concerning families, senior citizens and facilities for the disabled. You can find these and other booklets of hotel listings at Swiss National Tourist Offices abroad and at many travel agencies.

Tourist offices can tell you what type of accommodation is available (hotels of every category, pensions with full or partial board and apartment-hotels that offer a choice of rooms, studios or apartments).

Private rooms. Tourist offices will provide you with a list of rooms for rent in private homes – the Swiss equivalent of bed-and-breakfast. You can also knock on the door of houses that advertise a room to rent *(chambre à louer/Zimmer zu vermieten/camere da affitare)* outside.

Chalets and apartments. To rent a chalet or apartment, ask a travel agent at home or in Switzerland, check with the tourist information office (they have brochures for popular regions), or look in classified ads or on the Internet. Two good sites are Interhome <www.interhome.ch> and My Switzerland <www.myswitzerland.com>.

I would like a single/double room with bath/shower.

J'aimerais...	Ich möchte...	Vorrei...
une chambre à un	ein Einzelzimmer/	una camera
lit/deux lits	Doppelzimmer	singolo/doppia
avec bains/douche.	mit Bad/Dusche.	con bagno/doccia.

What is the rate per night?

Quel est le prix	Was kostet eine	Quanto costa per
pour une nuit?	Übernachtung?	notte?

AIRPORTS (aéroport/Flughafen/aeroporto)

Switzerland's three major international airports are, in order of importance: **Zurich-Kloten**, **Geneva-Cointrin** and **Basel/Mulhouse**. Swiss (formerly Swissair), the national carrier, provides frequent flights between these airports, and there are convenient rail connections as well. The airports of Bern and Lugano are smaller, but still offer some direct flights to other countries.

A train service makes the 10-minute trip from Zurich-Kloten airport to the city's main railway station four or five times an hour and every 10 minutes in peak periods. From Geneva-Cointrin, there are six departures an hour during peak time to the Gare Cornavin, the main railway station in the centre of Geneva, a six-minute trip. Trains also run four or five times an hour to Lausanne. The airports at Bern and Lugano provide shuttle bus connections to their appropriate city centres, with departures every half-hour (there are pickups at each airline). A bus connects Basel airport with the city centre several times an hour during peak hours and at least twice an hour at other times. **Fly-Rail baggage service.** If you're departing from Zurich, Geneva or Basel on a scheduled or charter flight, you can register baggage all the way to your final destination at many Swiss railway and postal bus stations. You will generally be required to drop off your baggage 24 hours in advance. Some large railway stations (23 in all) also have a check-in station and will issue you an airline boarding card (this is included in the price of sending your bags). The fee is well worth it, considering the hassle avoided. This service is also available upon your arrival in Switzerland.

B

BICYCLE HIRE (RENTAL)

For those who want to get in shape, Switzerland's terrain is rarely flat. You can hire a bicycle *(bicyclette/Velo/bicicletta)* at any major railway station (230 across the country) and return it (for a fee of

CHF6–12) to any other station that accepts bikes (ask in advance) during opening hours at the baggage counter. You will find leaflets describing special biking paths at tourist information offices.

BUDGETING FOR YOUR TRIP

Switzerland has a reputation as an expensive country. Given the strength of its currency and the extensive development of its tourism industry, prices are generally comparable to those in major tourist destinations elsewhere in Europe. Prices are higher in fashionable resorts, as well as in big cities such as Geneva and Zurich, but vary relatively little from one region to the next. To give you an idea, here are some average prices in Swiss francs (CHF).

Bus. CHF2.50 for a short trip; day passes CHF5–10.

Bicycle hire. CHF25–30 (24 hours).

Ski equipment hire. Cross-country CHF40+ per day, CHF150+ per week. Downhill skiing, CHF50+ per day, CHF200+ per week.

Meals and drinks. Breakfast CHF12, lunch (in a good restaurant) CHF25–40, daily special CHF20–30, dinner CHF45–60, fondue CHF20–30, coffee CHF3.50, draft beer (½ litre) CHF5, bottle of wine (½ litre) CHF20–30, non-alcoholic drinks CHF5.

Swiss Pass (second class, includes most mountain railways and lake steamers). CHF255 (4 days), CHF368 (8 days), CHF446 (15 days), CHF514 (22 days), CHF566 (1 month).

C

CAMPING

Several hundred campsites, some in the Alps, are approved by the Swiss Camping and Caravan Association (tel: 031 852 0626, <www.swisscamps.ch>). Ask for the Swiss camping guide at a local Swiss tourist office *(see page 172)*, at the Swiss Touring Club, Camping Division, Chemin de Blandonnet 4, 1214 Vernier (tel: 022 417 2727, <www.tcs.ch>), or at bookshops.

CAR HIRE (RENTAL)

To hire a car you must produce a valid driving licence, held for a minimum of one year. You must be at least 25 years old. You can hire a car at many railway stations. Agencies usually waive cash deposits for clients with recognised credit cards.

CLIMATE

In general, Switzerland's climate is continental. The winters are cold and snowy (especially in the mountains); the summers are hot with occasional storms. Spring tends to be cool and unpredictable, autumn usually stable and mild. All year, temperatures can vary considerably within a few hours, a few kilometres or a few hundred metres of altitude. It may be pouring rain in northern Switzerland and perfectly sunny in Ticino or Engadine. The chart shows the average daytime temperature in Geneva, month by month:

	J	F	M	A	M	J	J	A	S	O	N	D
°C	0	1	5	9	13	17	18	18	14	9	4	1
°F	32	34	41	48	55	63	65	65	57	48	39	34

CLOTHING

In view of the unpredictable weather patterns, it is best to be ready for anything. In summer, don't forget to take along a raincoat and umbrella, as well as a jacket or sweater. In winter, bring a warm coat and lined, waterproof snow boots for the mountains.

CRIME AND SAFETY (see also EMERGENCIES)

Muggings and violent crimes are rare in Switzerland, where you can generally come and go, day and night, in peace. Nevertheless it is always wise to lock your car and put your valuables in the hotel safe. In winter, keep your skis in a safe place: they can easily disappear from car roof-racks and the entrances to après-ski spots.

CUSTOMS AND ENTRY REQUIREMENTS

Most visitors – including citizens of the UK, the US, Canada and most other English-speaking countries – need only a valid passport to enter Switzerland. You are entitled to stay for up to 90 days without further formality. In 2005, Switzerland approved the Schengen Agreement, easing flow of travel between other Schengen countries in Europe with a special visa. Check with the Swiss embassy in your country for information on obtaining this visa.

You may take the following duty-free into Switzerland: 200 cigarettes or 50 cigars or 250g tobacco (European visitors), or 400 cigarettes or 100 cigars or 500g tobacco (non-European visitors), plus 1 litre spirits and 2 litres wine (either).

When returning to your own country you may take: **Australia:** 250 cigarettes or 250g of cigars or 250g tobacco, plus 2.25 litres of spirits and wine in total; **Canada:** 200 cigarettes and 50 cigars and 200g tobacco, plus 1.1 litres spirits or 1.5 litres wine; **Ireland:** 200 cigarettes or 50 cigars or 250g tobacco, plus 1 litre spirits or 2 litres wine; **New Zealand:** 200 cigarettes or 50 cigars or 250g tobacco, plus 1.125 litres spirits or 4.5 litres wine; **South Africa:** 200 cigarettes or 20 cigars or 250g tobacco, plus 1 litre spirits and 1 litre wine; **UK:** 200 cigarettes or 50 cigars or 250g tobacco, plus 1 litre spirits and 2 litres wine; **US:** 200 cigarettes and 100 cigars (no Cuban cigars) and a reasonable quantity of tobacco, plus 1 litre spirits or 1 litre wine.

Monetary restrictions. There is no restriction on the import or export of either Swiss or foreign currencies.

D

DRIVING (see also CAR HIRE)

To bring your car into Switzerland, you'll need a national driving licence, car registration papers and your Green Card (a recommended but not obligatory extension to your regular car insurance policy, validating it for foreign countries). A nationality code sticker must be visible at the rear of your car, and you must have a red warning triangle reflector for use in case of a breakdown. Seat belts are obligatory both in town and in the country. In winter you may be required to use snow chains on Alpine passes. These can be obtained at petrol stations along the way.

On the road. Drive on the right and give priority to the right unless otherwise indicated. On mountain roads, leave the awesome views to the passengers; to admire the scenery in safety, stop at roadside parking areas. On difficult stretches of mountain roads, right-of-way is given to postal buses or otherwise to the ascending vehicle. Honking your horn is recommended on blind corners of mountain roads; avoid it everywhere else. In general roads are good, and there is a well-developed motorway network linking all the big towns.

Autoroute tax. An annual road tax of CHF40 is levied on all cars and motorcycles using Swiss autoroutes. An additional fee of CHF40 applies to trailers and caravans. The *vignette* (sticker) is valid from 1 December of the year preceding the date stamped on the vignette to 31 January of the following year. It can be purchased from customs officers at border crossings or at any post office and is valid for multiple re-entry into Switzerland throughout its period of validity.

Speed limits. On the green signposted highways *(autoroute/ Autobahn/autostrada)*, the maximum speed is 120kph (75mph). On other roads the limit is 80kph (50mph) unless otherwise indicated. In residential areas the speed limit is generally restricted to 50kph (31mph), although you might encounter sections posted at either 60kph (37mph) or 30kph (19mph). Cars towing caravans and trailers may not exceed 80kph (50mph), even on highways.

Car trouble. If your car breaks down, call the TCS or Swiss Touring Club *(Touring Club Suisse/Touring-Club Schweiz/Touring Club Svizzero,* tel: 0844 888111). It is also a good idea to contact an international insurance company before leaving to cover costs, otherwise, you will be responsible for the full price of paying a mechanic or tow truck. You can get help at any public telephone by dialling 140. Emergency telephones are installed at regular intervals along motorways.

driving licence		
permis de conduire	*Führerausweis*	*licenza di condurre*
car registration papers		
carte grise/permis de circulation	*Fahrzegausweis*	*licenza di circolazione*
Fill the tank, please.		
Le plein, s'il vous plaît.	*Volltanken, bitte.*	*Il pieno, per favore.*
I've had a breakdown.		
Ma voiture est en panne.	*Ich habe eine Panne.*	*Io avuto un guasto.*
There has been an accident.		
Il y a eu un accident.	*Es ist ein Unfall passiert.*	*C'è stato un incidente.*

Parking. Try to avoid parking in congested central shopping zones or historic city centres. Most cities have adopted a system of parking meters or blue zones *(zone bleu/Blaue Zona/zona blu)* and red zones *(zone rouge/Rote Zone/zona rossa)*, which limit parking time to, respectively, 1½ hours and 15 hours. To park in these zones, marked with blue or red paint, you must display a parking disc *(disc de stationnement, Parkscheibe/disco orario)* on the dashboard indicating when you left your car (some blue zones require a paid parking sticker). The parking discs are given out free of charge at petrol stations, banks and police stations. Paid carparks are also widely available. Rarely seen 'white zones' allow for unlimited parking.

Road signs. Most signs in Switzerland conform to international norms. Here are the translations for some common signs:

exit	sortie	*Ausfahrt*	*uscita*
airport	aéroport	*Flughafen*	*aeroporto*
icy road	verglas	*Glatteis*	*strada ghiacitta*
city centre	centre-ville	*Stadtzentrum*	*centro città*
detour	deviation	*Umleitung*	*deviazione*
customs	douane	*Zoll*	*dogana*

E

EMBASSIES AND CONSULATES
(Ambassade, Consulat/ Botschaft, Konsulate/Ambasciata, Consolato)

All embassies, located in Bern, have their own consular sections. Some countries also have consulates in Geneva, Zurich and other cities.

Australia: Consulate General: Chemin des Fins 2, PO Box 172, 1211 Geneva 19, tel: 022 799 9100, <www.australia.ch>.

Canada: Kirchenfeldstrasse 88, 3005 Bern, tel: 031 357 3200, <www.canada-ambassade.ch>.

Ireland: Kirchenfeldstrasse 68, 3005 Bern, tel: 031 352 1442. Zurich consulate: Claridenstrasse 25, PO Box 562, 8027 Zurich, tel: 044 289 2515.

New Zealand: Mission and Consulate General: Chemin des Fins 2, PO Box 334, 1211 Geneva, tel: 022 929 0350.

South Africa: Alpenstrasse 29, 3006 Bern, tel: 031 350 1313.

UK: Thunstrasse 50, 3005 Bern, tel: 031 359 7700, <www.british embassy.ch>.

Geneva consulate: Rue de Vermont 37–39, PO Box 67, 1211 Geneva, tel: 022 918 2400.

Vice-Consulate: Hegibachstrasse 47, 8032 Zurich, tel: 044 383 6560.

US: Jubiläumsstrasse 93, 3005 Bern, tel: 031 357 7011, 031 357 7234, <http://bern.usembassy.gov>.

Geneva consulate: Rue Versonnex 7, 1207 Geneva, tel: 022 840 5160.

Zurich consulate: Dufourstrasse 101, 8008 Zurich, tel: 043 499 2960.

EMERGENCIES *(urgences/Notfall /emergenza)*

Police	**117**
Fire	**118**
Roadside assistance	**140**
Paramedics, ambulance	**144**

For a chemist, doctor or dentist on 24-hour duty, consult the daily local paper. The addresses of chemists open on Sundays and holidays are posted in the window of other branches.

G

GETTING THERE

By air. From Great Britain and Ireland. There are frequent daily flights from London to Basel, Zurich and Geneva, several to Bern and two a day to Lugano via Bern. You can also fly to Zurich and Geneva from Manchester and Birmingham. There are one or two flights a day from Dublin to Zurich and several a week to Geneva.

From North America. There are several direct flights a day from New York to Zurich and Geneva, and a few to Basel with connections. There is at least one flight a day from Montreal and Toronto to Zurich.

From the southern hemisphere. From Australia and New Zealand you can catch daily flights to Switzerland with one change. There is at least one flight a day from South Africa.

Internal flights. Air shuttles link Geneva with Zurich (45 mins, 10+ flights a day) and Lugano (55 mins, several flights a day). There are many daily flights between Bern and Lugano (45 mins), Zurich and Lugano (50 mins), and Zurich and Basel (30 mins). FlyBaboo (<www.flybaboo.com>), Swiss (<www.swiss.com>) and Darwin Airline (<www.darwinairline.com>) run many of these connections.

Discounts and special fares. Offers vary from one travel agent or airline to another. Ask about special fares. Swiss consulates abroad can guide you to agencies specialising in travel to Switzerland.

Package trips. There are many options for fixed-price travel. Packages may include your flight, hotel or apartment and car hire, *à la carte* trips, trips with train fares and hotel included, driving trips and 'theme' trips (art, sports etc). Ask your travel agent for details.

By rail. The journey from **London** to Paris aboard the Eurostar high-speed train (TGV or *train à grande vitesse*, tel: 08705 186 186, <www.eurostar.com>) takes 2 hours 10 minutes via the Channel Tunnel. It then takes another 4 hours by TGV to get to Switzerland. Check arrival and departure locations in Paris, as you may have to change stations there.

From Paris. There are five or six TGVs a day to Geneva and four or five to Lausanne. There is one direct TGV a day from Paris to Bern, or you can take one of several daily trains and change in Basel or Geneva. To get from Paris to Zurich you'll have to change at least once. There are also several trains between Paris and Evian. Paris to Basel trains leave several times a day, and there is one direct train between Nice and Geneva.

From Spain. There are trains from Barcelona to Geneva, including a night train (Trainhotel), which goes on to Lausanne and Zurich.

By road. The itineraries noted here, usually on highways, are the fastest and most comfortable routes. Travel time corresponds to the average trip taken in normal traffic conditions. You can also contact your country's Touring Club before travelling for more detailed information.

Book your passage on **car ferries** well in advance. Fares are cheaper for midweek sailings, and the price fluctuates seasonally. The best route is Calais–Reims–Chaumont–Basel–Zurich or Calais/Bologne–Paris–Geneva.

There are regular **coach** services between London's Victoria Station and Basel, Bern, Geneva and Zurich. These trips take roughly 18 hours (go to <www.nationalexpress.com> for information).

From Belgium. From Brussels to Geneva via Sterpenich (A6), Bourg-en-Bresse (A39) and St-Julien (A40/A401) is 812km/508 miles (8 hours 50 minutes). Between Brussels and Zurich via Luxembourg, Sterpenich (A6), Strasbourg (A4) and Basel–St-Louis is a total of 665km/415 miles (7 hours 40 minutes).

From France. Paris and Geneva are 535km/335 miles (6 hours 10 minutes) apart via Beaune-Nord (A6/A31) and St-Julien (A40-A401). From Paris to Lausanne is a trip of 535km/335 miles (6 hours 20 minutes) via Beaune-Nord (A6/A31) and Vallorbe (A9). Paris/Zurich is a distance of 650km/406 miles via Beaune-Nord (A6/A31), Belfort (A36) and Mulhouse/Basel–St-Louis (A2). Nice/Geneva: 545km/340 miles (6 hours 40 minutes) via Menton/Grimaldi (A8/A10), Turin (A5), Aosta, Annemasse (A40) and Thonex. From Nice, Digne and Sisteron, you can also reach Geneva by the Napoleon highway (Gap) or the Alpen route (Croix-Haute pass) in Grenoble; take the A41 highway to the border of Switzerland.

H

HEALTH AND MEDICAL CARE

Most major tourist resorts have clinics, and all cities are served by modern, well-equipped hospitals. The standard of treatment is high. For less serious ailments, a chemist *(pharmacie/Apotheke/farmacia)* will dispense medication and suggest a doctor if necessary.

EU citizens should get a European Health Insurance Card (EHIC), available from post offices or online, entitling them to reduced-cost, or free, medical treatment. To cover all eventualities a travel insurance policy is advisable, and for non-EU residents, essential.

I need a doctor/a dentist.
Il me faut un   Ich brauche einen   *Ho bisogno di un*
    médecin/un dentiste.   Arzt/einen Zahnarzt.   *medico/un dentista.*

L

LANGUAGE

Switzerland has four national languages: German, French, Italian and Romansh. Swiss German or Schwyzerdütsch, spoken by nearly two-thirds of the population (in the country's north and centre), groups a number of dialects which are often incomprehensible to a speaker of High German. Hochdeutsch or literary German, which German-speaking Swiss learn at school, is like a foreign tongue to them.

Italian is spoken only in Ticino (in the south) and parts of Grisons. Scwyzerdütsch and Romansh are also spoken in parts of these regions. Romansh comes from low Latin and has several dialects. French is spoken mainly in the west of the country but is understood everywhere.

The Swiss tend to be good at learning foreign languages and often speak two, three or even four languages. Many people speak English well enough to help you find your way around.

When you enter an office or shop, remember the Swiss German expression *Grüzi (mitenand)*, which means roughly 'Good morning (everyone)'. In Italian, you can say *buon giorno* (good morning) or *buona sera* ('good evening'). When you leave, say *adieu (mitenand)* or *arrivederci* if you are in Ticino. In response, you may hear *Uf wiederluege* ('until next time') or *a presto* ('until soon').

Do you speak English?
Parlez-vous anglais?   *Sprechen Sie Englisch?*   **Parla inglese?**
Help me, please.
Aidez-moi, s'il vous plaît.   *Helfen Sie mir, bitte.*   **Mi aiuti, per favore.**
I don't understand.
Je ne comprends pas.   *Ich verstehe nicht.*   **Non capisco.**
Could you speak more slowly?
Pourriez-vous parler   *Könnten Sie langsamer*   **Potrebbe parlare**
  plus lentement?   *sprechen?*   **più lentamente?**

good morning	bonjour	*guten Tag*	**buon giorno**
good evening	bonsoir	*guten Abend*	**buona sera**
good night	bonne nuit	*gute Nacht*	**buona notte**
goodbye	au revoir	*auf Wiedersehen*	**arrivederci**
yes/no	oui/non	*ja/nein*	**sì/no**
please	s'il vous plaît	*bitte*	**per favore**
thank you	merci	*danke*	**grazie**
when/where	quand/où	*wann/wo*	**quando/dove**
how	comment	*wie*	**come**
yesterday	hier	*gestern*	**ieri**
today	aujourd'hui	*heute*	**oggi**
tomorrow	demain	*morgen*	**domani**
day/week	jour/semaine	*Tag/Woche*	**giorno/settimana**
month/year	mois/année	*Monat/Jahr*	**mese/anno**
left/right	gauche/droite	*links/rechts*	**sinistra/destra**
high/low	en haut/en bas	*oben/unten*	**sopra/sotto**
good/bad	bon/mauvais	*gut/schlecht*	**buono/cattivo**
big/small	grand/petit	*gross/klein*	**grande/piccolo**
cold/hot	froid/chaud	*kalt/heiss*	**freddo/caldo**
old/new	vieux/neuf	*alt/neu*	**vecchio/nuovo**
open/closed	ouvert/fermé	*offen/geschlossen*	**aperto/chiuso**
free/occupied	libre/occupé	*frei/besetzt*	**libero/occupato**
early/late	tôt/tard	*früh/spät*	**presto/tardi**
easy/hard	facile/difficile	*einfach/schwierig*	**facile/difficile**

LOST PROPERTY

If you have lost something, check first with your hotel reception desk, then report the loss to the nearest police station. Every city has a lost property office *(bureau d'objets trouvés/Fundbüro/ Ufficio oggetti smarriti)*.

You can reclaim articles left behind on trains or buses at the railway or public transport lost property office.

> **I have lost my wallet/my handbag/my passport.**
>
> | J'ai perdu mon | Ich habe mein | Ho perso il |
> |---|---|---|
> | porte-monnaie/ | Portemonnaie/ | portafoglio/ |
> | mon sac à main/ | meine Handtasche/ | la borsetta/ |
> | mon passeport. | meinen Pass verloren. | il passaporto. |

M

MAPS

Bookshops, stationery shops and some newspaper stands offer a wide selection of road and regional maps, as well as city maps. Tourist offices, car-hire agencies and the larger banks distribute excellent city maps.

Hikers will find indispensable topographical maps at local or regional tourist offices. Switzerland's well-maintained footpaths are also well-marked with yellow blazes and signposts that display the average time for a given hike.

> **city map**
>
> | un plan de ville | ein Stadtplan | una pianta della città |
> |---|---|---|
> | **road map** | | |
> | une carte routière | eine Strassenkarte | una carta stradale |

MEDIA

Newspapers. Even in small towns, newsstands stock a surprisingly wide variety of foreign papers, plus all the Swiss newspapers. The best selection and earliest delivery are offered by main railway stations and airports. English-language daily newspapers such as the *International Herald Tribune*, *USA Today*, *Wall Street Journal Europe* and *European Financial Times* are available on the day of publication.

Magazines and books. There are several monthly magazines published in Switzerland, including *Swiss News* and *Earth Focus*. English-language magazines of all kinds are widely available across the country. In most large towns you will find English-language bookshops. Any serious bookshop will offer at least a small selection of English-language paperbacks.

Television and radio. There are four Swiss cable TV stations (in French, German and Italian, which can be tuned in without cable as well), plus German, Austrian and Italian stations. Some of the programmes are dual-language broadcasts, showing films in French, German or Italian and the original language, very often English. English-language cable TV stations include CNBC Europe, CNN International, Eurosport, MTV Europe and BBC World. Cable radio stations usually include BBC World Service and BBC Foreign Language Service, Sky Radio, Voice of America and Swiss Radio International English Service (online service at <www.swissinfo.org>) plus a number of FM stations from Switzerland (both local, like World Radio in Geneva, and national). Depending where you are, you might pick up stations from Germany, Austria, France or Italy.

MONEY MATTERS

Currency. The monetary unit of Switzerland is the Swiss franc *(franc suisse/Schweizer Franken/franco svizzero)*, which is usually abbreviated as CHF or SFr. It is divided into 100 centimes *(Rappen/centesini)*, abbreviated Rp. in German and ct. in French or Italian. **Coins:** 5, 10, 20 and 50 centimes; 1, 2 and 5 francs (the latter is often called *cent sous*). **Notes:** 10, 20, 50, 100, 200 and 1,000 francs.

Banks. Most banks are open weekdays 8.30am–12.30pm and 1.30–4.30, 5 or 5.30pm. Main branches generally remain open during lunch hour. One day a week, branches stay open until 6 or 6.30pm. Currency exchange offices at airports and the larger railway stations do business from around 6.30am–7.30pm every day. There is no charge to change Swiss or foreign money, buy or sell traveller's cheques in different currencies or cash Eurocheques. Cashpoints or ATM machines can be found nearly everywhere and accept all cards in the EU network.

Credit cards. Smaller businesses, particularly in remote regions or small villages, may not accept credit cards, but they are widely accepted in major establishments and in large cities.

Traveller's cheques. The well-known international cheques are generally accepted everywhere. The exchange rate for traveller's cheques is better in banks than elsewhere. You must show your passport when cashing a traveller's cheque.

Do you accept traveller's cheques?

Acceptez-vous les chèques de voyage?	Nehmen Sie Reiseschecks?	Accetta assegni turistici?

Can I pay with a credit card?

Puis-je payer avec cette carte de crédit?	Kann ich mit dieser Kreditkarte bezahlen?	Posso pagare con questa carta di credito?

O

OPENING HOURS (see also PUBLIC HOLIDAYS)

Most offices are open 8am–noon and 1.30 or 2–5pm (sometimes 6pm), Monday to Friday.

Department stores and most other shops open at 8am (some at 8.30 or 9am) until 6.30 or 7pm. Some neighbourhood or village grocery stores open at 7am and close for lunch, as do most boutiques, except in the larger cities. In some cities, closing time is extended until 9pm one night a week. Some businesses close for a half-day during the week – often Monday morning or Wednesday,

Thursday or Saturday afternoon. On Saturdays, many shops open 8am–4, 5 or 5.30pm, depending on the region. On Sundays, everything closes except for a few food stores (which stay open all or part of the day). In ski resorts during the high season, boutiques are open all week.

Museum hours vary, but in general they are open to the public from Tuesday to Sunday 10am–noon and 2–5 or 6pm. Large museums and museums in big cities generally stay open through lunch.

(See page 164 for banks and below for post offices.)

P

POLICE *(police/Polizei/polizia)*

Switzerland does not have a uniformed federal police. Law and order is the responsibility of the individual cantons and communities, so police uniforms vary greatly from one place to the next. Police are armed, efficient and courteous. Law enforcement is strict.

The emergency telephone number for the police is **117**.

Where is the nearest police station?

Où est le poste de police le plus proche?	Wo ist die nächste Polizeiwache?	*Dove si trova il posto di polizia più vicino?*

POST OFFICES *(bureau de poste/ Post/ufficio postale)*

In addition to normal postal business, post offices handle telegrams and bill-paying. They are generally open from 7.30am until noon and from 1.30pm until 6 or 6.30pm, depending on the size of the office, and from 7.30 to 11am on Saturdays. In big cities, major post office stays open at lunchtime, and a window reserved for urgent mail stays open until 10pm, sometimes later. In smaller towns, hours may vary.

You can also buy stamps at machines outside the post office or at the railway station, newsstands, tobacco shops, souvenir shops (since they sell postcards) or at the hotel. Swiss mailboxes are yellow.

If you don't know in advance where you will be staying in Switzerland, you can have your mail addressed to the general delivery desk *(poste restante/postlagernd/fermo posta)* at the main post office of any town you expect to visit.

express mail	par exprès	*Express*	**espresso**
registered	en recommandé	*eingeschrieben*	**raccomandata**
a stamp	un timbre	*eine Briefmarke*	**un francobollo**

PUBLIC HOLIDAYS *(jours fériés/gesetzliche Feiertage/feste)*

The holiday calendar varies from one canton to the next, according to the local history and religious traditions. Here are the official Swiss holidays, observed all over the country unless noted otherwise:

New Year (1 Jan)	Nouvel An	*Neujahr*	**Capodanno**
Good Friday	Vendredi-Saint	*Karfreitag*	**Venerdi Santo**
Easter Monday*	Lundi de Páques	*Ostermontag*	**Lunedì di Pasqua**
Ascension Day	Ascension	*Auffahrt*	**Ascensione**
Monday of Pentecost*	Lundi de Pentecôte	*Pfingstmontag*	**Lunedi di Pentecoste**
Swiss National Day (1 Aug)	Fête national	*Bundesfeier*	**Festa nazionale**
Christmas (25 Dec)	Noël	*Weihnachten*	**Natale**
St Stephen's Day* (26 Dec)	Saint-Etienne	*Stefanstag*	**Santo Stefano**

*Holidays celebrated in nearly all cantons

On these holidays, banks and stores stay closed all day; the same is true for 1 May in certain cantons. Catholic cantons also observe the day of the Immaculate Conception (8 December).

PUBLIC TRANSPORT

Train *(see also page 159)*. Both the Swiss Federal Railways (CFF/SBB/FFS; <www.rail.ch>) and smaller private railways live up to the Swiss reputation: fast, clean, comfortable and punctual, although heavy snowfalls may cause delays. Trains run at regular intervals, with an hourly service generally provided between all major cities. Intercity trains are air-conditioned, with first- and second-class cars. In addition they offer 'family cars', equipped with game rooms where children can play during the trip, and 'quiet cars'. Direct trains *(train direct/Schnellzug/treno diretto)* are express trains serving major cities and medium-sized towns. Regional trains *(train régional/Regionalzug/treno regionale)* are local trains making all station stops.

Timetables are posted in every station, and listed connecting trains are always guaranteed. Tickets can be bought from ticket windows or automatic machines and will be punched on the train by an inspector.

There are several systems of passes good for train travel throughout Switzerland: The **Eurailpass** in all its categories (Eurail Youthpass, Eurail Saverpass, Eurail Flexipass, Eurail Flexipass Youth and Eurail Saver Flexipass) is available only to non-European residents. It is issued in the holder's home country (<www.raileurope.com>).

The **Inter Rail** pass comes in three categories according to age (adults, under 26 and children ages 4–11). A fourth category, the Euro Domino option, is specially designed for people living in Europe, including Switzerland. These are available at all railway stations, many travel agencies or online at <www.raileurope.co.uk>.

The **Swiss Travel System** (STS) offers two excellent deals, the Swiss Pass and the Swiss Card, for individual trips that combine several different means of transport. These practical and economical tickets are available to anyone living outside Switzerland. The **Swiss Pass** allows unrestricted rail, postal bus or boat travel for periods of 4, 8, 15 or 22 days or one month. Trams and buses in many cities are also included, as are discounts of 25 percent on most mountain trains and panoramic routes. The **Swiss Youth Pass** (under 26) gives a 25 percent discount on the price of the Swiss Pass. The **Swiss Flexipass** is valid for travel on any three to six or eight days within one month and includes the same reductions that are available with the Swiss Pass. The **Swiss Card** offers you one month of half-price travel by train, postal bus or boat (including a special discount of 25–50 percent on most mountain trains), in addition to free round-trip connections between the airport or border train station and the town you are travelling to). With the **Family Pass**, children under 16 accompany their parents free.

Apply for the passes at travel agencies or Swiss tourist offices abroad. You can also get STS passes in any of Switzerland's major railway stations, (bring your passport). For more details contact Swiss Railway SBB, Hochschulstrasse 6, CH3000 Bern 65, tel: +41 (0)900 300 300, <www.rail.ch>; or the Swiss Federal Railways Travel Bureau at Zurich or Geneva airports; or visit <www.myswitzerland.raileurope.com>, which also provides information on many Swiss scenic trains. *(See also pages 152 and 172–3.)*

Postal bus. Wherever the trains don't go, the bright yellow postal buses do. They carry mail and passengers over mountain roads to the smallest of hamlets. Their trustworthy drivers have been trained to manoeuvre on the most fearsome mountain roads in any weather.

Connections between trains and postal buses are scheduled for convenience. You can buy tickets at the train station, on the bus or sometimes at the post office (tel: 0848 888 888, <www.postbus.ch>).

Boat. Switzerland's great lakes are all crisscrossed by sizeable passenger boats, often with paddle-wheels. Many have their own restaurants. From Lausanne, the Lake of Geneva *(Lac Léman)* ferries are the fastest way to get to France (frequent departures every day for Evian). There are also daily tours around the lake from June to September. Every Sunday in winter, a boat makes the round-trip journey from Lausanne to Vevey, Montreux, Villeneuve and St-Gingolphe.

Bus or tram. All Swiss cities have efficient public transport networks (bus, trolley-bus or tram). Tickets are available from machines at each stop. You can sometimes by them on board, although that will usually be more expensive. Be sure to hold on to your ticket, as they are frequently checked by roving conductors. You can also buy books of 10 tickets or 24-hour passes *(carte de 24 heures/Tageskarte/abbonamento giornaliero)*; ask at major bus stops or newsstands.

Taxi. You can always hail a passing taxi, but on rainy days, it might be a better bet to head directly to a cab stand (on major squares or around railway stations) or to reserve by phone. Though fares vary from city to city, they are always high. All taxis have a meter and a table listing additional charges for extras such as baggage. Tips are generally included in the price *(see Tipping)*.

first/second class		
première/seconde classe	erste/zweite Klasse	*prima/seconda classe*
one-way/return (round trip)		
aller simple/aller-retour	einfach/retour	*andata/andata e ritorno*
Where is the nearest bus stop?		
Où est l'arrêt de bus le plus proche?	Wo ist die nächste Bushaltestelle?	*Dovè si trova la fermata d'autobus più vicina?*

R

RELIGION

Switzerland is almost equally divided between Roman Catholics and Protestants, but they are unevenly spread among the cantons. In big cities, many other religions are represented as well.

The hours of church services *(cultes/Gottesdienst/culto)* and Mass *(messe/Mess/missa)* are often posted as you enter villages and small towns. Elsewhere, look in the daily papers or at tourist offices.

T

TELEPHONES *(téléphone/Telefon/telefono)*

Public phone booths can be used for direct international calls. To use the majority of public phones you will need a *Taxcard*, a magnetic calling card available at post offices and newsstands. You can also use Visa, Eurocard or American Express.

TIME ZONE

Switzerland is on Central European Time, which is Greenwich Mean Time +1 hour. In summer, Daylight Savings Time is applied at the same dates as in neighbouring countries.

TIPPING *(pourboire/Trinkgeld /mancia)*

Tips are generally included in the bill, but for exceptional service, you may round off the total or leave an extra 5 percent. Porters will expect a coin. Taxi drivers also get a tip, usually around 10 percent.

TOILETS

Public toilets are clean and easily accessible, sometimes with a small charge. They are marked *Mesdames* (in French), *Damen/Frauen* (in Swiss German) or *signore/donne* (in Ticino) for women, and *Messieurs*, *Herren/Männer* or *signori/uomini*, for men.

TOURIST INFORMATION

In major cities throughout the world, you will find a Swiss National Tourist Office to assist with the planning of your trip.
UK and Ireland: Switzerland Tourism, Swiss Centre, 30 Bedford Street, London WC2E 9ED, tel: 00800 1002 0030, email: <info. uk@myswitzerland.com>.
US and Canada: Switzerland Tourism, 608 Fifth Avenue, New York, NY 10020, tel: 1-877 794 8037 or 011800-100-200-30, email: <info.usa@myswitzerland.com>.

In Switzerland itself, the head branch of the Swiss National Tourist Office is located at Tödistrasse 7, CH-8027 Zurich, tel: 044 288 1111 or 008 00100 20030, <www.myswitzerland.com>. This website has a great deal of information on the many different regions in Switzerland.

Every region, city and resort has its own tourist office *(office de tourisme/Verkehrsburo* or *Verkehrsverein/ente per il turismo)*, with free brochures, lists of hotels and maps.

Here are some of them:

Basel	Steinenberg 14, CH-4001 Basel, tel: 061 268 6868, <www.baseltourismus.ch>.
Bellinzona and Ticino	Via Lugano 12, CH-6501 Bellinzona, tel: 091 825 7056, <www.ticino.ch>.
Bern	Im Bahnhof, Postfach, 3001 Bern, tel: 031 328 1212, <www.berninfo.com>.
Chur	Grabenstrasse 5, 7002 Chur, tel: 081 252 1818, <www.churtourismus.ch>.
Fribourg	Avenue de la Gare 1, CH-1701 Fribourg, tel: 026 350 1111, <www.fribourgtourism.ch>.
Geneva	Rue du Mont-Blanc 18, CH-1211 Geneva, tel: 022 909 7000, <www.geneve-tourisme.ch>.
Interlaken	Höheweg 37, CH-3800 Interlaken, tel: 033 826 5300, <www.interlaken.ch>.
Lake Geneva	Avenue d'Ouchy 60, CH-1000 Lausanne 6-Ouchy, tel: 021 613 2626, <www.lake-geneva-region.ch>.
Lausanne	Place de la Navigation 4, CH-1006 Lausanne-Ouchy, tel: 021 613 7373, <www.lausanne-tourisme.ch>.
Lucerne	Zentralstrasse 5, CH-6002 Luzern, tel: 041 227 1717, <www.luzern.org>.
Lugano	Palazzo Civico-Riva Albertolli, CP 6080, CH-6901 Lugano, tel: 091 913 3232, <www.lugano-tourism.ch>.
Neuchâtel	Hôtel des Postes, CH-2001 Neuchâtel, tel: 032 889 6890, <www.neuchateltourisme.ch>.

St-Gallen	Bahnhofplatz 1A, CH-9001 St Gallen, tel: 071 227 3737, <www.st.gallen-bodensee.ch>.
Saignelégier and Jura	Jura Tourism, 6 Place du 23 Juin, CH-2350 Saigne-légier, tel: 032 420 4770, <www.juratourisme.ch>.
Sion	Place de la Planta, CH-1950 Sion, tel: 027 327 7727, <www.siontourism.ch>.
Valais	Rue Pré-Fleuri 6, CH-1951 Sion, tel: 027 327 3570, <www.valaistourism.ch>.
Zurich	Im Hauptbahnhof, CH-8023 Zürich, tel: 044 215 4000, <www.zuerich.com>.

W

WEBSITES

www.myswitzerland.com Swiss tourism.

www.swissinfo.org, **www.swissworld.org** General information and news.

www.swisshotels.ch Booking site for hotels and inns.

www.romantikhotels.ch, **www.relaischateaux.com** Hotel group sites with several unique hotels and inns in Switzerland.

www.gstaad.ch, **www.interlaken.ch**, **www.stmoritz.ch**, **www. verbier.ch**, **www.zermatt.ch** Regional resort sites with informa-tion on accommodation and snow reports.

Y

YOUTH HOSTELS
(auberge de jeunesse/Jugendherberge/ostello della gioventù)

There is no age limit for youth hostels, but those under 25 have priority. Reservations are recommended during the high season. For a complete list of hostels and their rules, write to: Swiss Youth Hostels, Schaffhauserstrasse 14, CH-8042 Zurich, tel: 044 360 1414, <www.youthhostel.ch>.

Recommended Hotels

The following hotels in cities and resorts throughout Switzerland are listed alphabetically. Consider making reservations well in advance, particularly in the winter resorts from late December through till March. Many hotels in resort towns will require a seven-night minimum stay during the high season.

Prices normally include all taxes, but some will have an extra service charge or city tax. Breakfast is often included. Low-season rates can be much lower and, in many of the big cities, there are often reduced weekend rates. Also note, all Basel hotels come with a mobility ticket providing free public transport during your visit. These symbols represent an approximate guide in Swiss Francs for a double room with bath or shower during the high season.

$$$$$	over CHF450
$$$$	CHF300–450
$$$	CHF200–300
$$	CHF150–200
$	below CHF150

APPENZELL

Romantik Hotel Säntis $$–$$$ *Landsgemeindeplatz, tel: 071 788 1111, fax: 071 788 1110, <www.saentis-appenzell.ch>*. This small, family-run hotel with a beautiful façade enjoys a prominent location on Appenzell's main square. Modern rooms, but some can be noisy if facing the *Platz*. The hotel's restaurant offers excellent regional cuisine and good wine at reasonable prices. 37 rooms.

BASEL

Der Teufelhof Basel $$$–$$$$ *Leonhardsgraben 47–49, tel: 061 261 1010, fax: 061 261 1004, <www.teufelhof.com>*. Art and theatre are the focus here as two small hotels are combined with a small theatre. The Art Hotel has eight rooms and a suite, each individually designed. The Gallery Hotel consists of 24 rooms in a former convent where artists exhibit their work. The small theatre is usually open during the winter months. There are two restaurants and a gourmet food and wine cellar.

Hotel Basel $$$–$$$$ *Münzgasse 12, tel: 061 264 6800, fax: 061 264 6811, <www.hotel-basel.ch>.* A well-maintained, business-orientated hotel with an efficient and courteous staff, located in the heart of the old town. Modern, spacious rooms, and a variety of suites also available. 72 rooms.

Hotel Brasserie Au Violon $–$$ *Im Lohnhof 4, tel: 061 269 8711, fax: 061 269 8712, <www.au-violon.com>.* For a unique experience, stay at this former prison in a quiet courtyard just above the old town. Renovated to keep a Spartan feel, the rooms are a bit small with low doorways, but clean. You can also stay in the former police station with views over the city. Popular French brasserie by the lobby. 20 rooms.

Hotel Krafft $$ *Rheingasse 12, tel: 061 690 9130, fax: 061 690 9131, <www.hotelkrafft.ch>.* In a building dating from 1872 overlooking the Rhine, all rooms have recently undergone renovation. Many have excellent views of the old town and Münster, some with a terrace. 45 rooms.

BERN

Belle Epoque $$$$ *Gerechtigkeitsgasse 18, tel: 031 311 4336, fax: 031 311 3936, <www.belle-epoque.ch>.* Situated in the lower part of the old town on one of Bern's most famous streets and just across the bridge from the Bear Pit. This small, charming hotel offers a quiet retreat in tastefully decorated rooms, most with antiques and furnishings from the Belle Epoque. 17 rooms.

Bellevue Palace $$$$$ *Kochergasse 3–5, tel: 031 320 4545, fax: 031 311 4743, <www.bellevue-palace.ch>.* Having hosted many dignitaries past and present from around the world, the Bellevue Palace is one of Bern's and Switzerland's top hotels. Old-world charm combines with modern conveniences: the guest rooms were renovated in 2002, and most of them have commanding views of the Alps. Excellent terrace restaurant with Alpine views. 130 rooms.

Hotel Bern $$$ *Zeughausgasse 9, tel: 031 329 2222, fax: 031 329 2299, <www.hotelbern.ch>*. A conveniently located hotel, just a short walk from the railway station. Recently remodelled rooms. Caters to a business clientele. 100 rooms.

Hotel Jardin $–$$ *Militärstrasse 38, tel: 031 333 0117, fax: 031 333 0943, <www.hotel-jardin.ch>*. In a quiet neighbourhood, just outside of the town centre. Inexpensive option with decent rooms. 18 rooms.

BIEL

Hotel Elite $$$ *rue de la Gare 14, tel: 032 328 7777, fax: 032 328 7770, <www.hotelelite.ch>*. An art deco hotel in a 1930s building with recently renovated rooms. Not far from the station. 74 rooms.

CRANS-MONTANA

Hostellerie du Pas de l'Ours $$$$$ *tel: 027 485 9333, fax: 027 485 9334, <www.pasdelours.ch>*. Nestling in the popular ski region of Crans-Montana, this Relais and Chateaux chalet offers nine suites with mountain ambience. Indoor and outdoor pools with other wellness options. Closed several months in the late spring and autumn.

DAVOS

Hotel Europe $$$ *Promenade 63, tel: 081 415 4141, fax: 081 415 4111, <www.europe-davos.ch>*. Well-equipped and located hotel near ski lifts. Rooms are average but adequate for the price. It has an indoor pool, sauna, several bars and restaurants. 64 rooms.

GENEVA

Des Bergues $$$$$ *quai des Bergues 33, tel: 022 908 7000, fax: 022 908 7400, <www.fourseasons.com/geneva>*. One of Geneva's oldest hotels, established on the right bank of the lake in 1834, this hotel was recently purchased and renovated by the Four Seasons group. It continues to be one of the great hotels in Geneva. The public rooms are splendid, and guest rooms are large and tastefully decorated. 103 rooms.

Domaine de Châteauvieux $$$ *chemin de Châteauvieux 16, Satigny, tel: 022 753 1511, fax: 022 753 1924, <www.chateau vieux.ch>*. Positioned among the rolling vineyards just outside of Geneva, this charming villa offers a quiet place to relax and enjoy the Swiss countryside and the Geneva wine country. Just a short drive to the heart of the city. 14 rooms.

Hôtel Central $ *rue de la Rôtisserie 2, tel: 022 818 8100, fax: 022 818 8101, <www.hotelcentral.ch>*. A hard-to-find, great-value hotel at the base of old town Geneva. Very basic rooms, but for the price, the location cannot be beaten. Rooms can be a bit small, but even the larger rooms are still very affordable. Reception is on the sixth floor. 40 rooms.

Hôtel Longemalle $$$ *place Longemalle 13, tel: 022 818 6262, fax: 022 818 6261, <www.longemalle.ch>*. On the left bank and in the centre of it all, Longemalle provides a nice alternative to its higher-priced competitors. Offering a great location (a short walk to old town and the lake), good service, and well-appointed rooms. 58 rooms.

Hôtel Tiffany $$$$ *rue des Marbriers 1, tel: 022 708 1616, fax: 022 708 1617, <www.hotel-tiffany.ch>*. A little off the beaten path, but still just a short walk to the heart of Geneva, this boutique hotel lies in a 19th-century building. The Parisian bistro keeps in tune with the ambiance of the hotel and offers excellent fare. 46 rooms.

GSTAAD

Grand Hotel Bellevue $$$$$ *tel: 033 748 0000, fax: 033 748 0001, <www.bellevue-gstaad.ch>*. Reopened in 2002 after a long renovation, this is one of Gstaad's finest and most popular hotels. Offers top-notch service and an extensive wellness centre with much to offer for relaxation. It also has several good dining options. 57 rooms.

INTERLAKEN

Hotel Interlaken $$$–$$$$ *Höheweg 74, tel: 033 826 6868, fax: 033 826 6869, <www.interlakenhotel.ch>.* A historic hotel, the oldest in town, which counts Lord Byron as one of its previous guests. The inside has been renovated and lacks charm, but the rooms are adequate and modern. 60 rooms.

Hotel Lötschberg $–$$ *General Guisan Strasse 31, tel: 033 822 2545, fax: 033 822 2579, <www.lotschberg.ch>.* Basic, comfortable rooms. An excellent-value, family-run hotel with a very attentive and helpful staff. They can help you plan many outdoor activities. 19 rooms.

LAUSANNE

Beau-Rivage Palace $$$$$ *place du Port 17–19, tel: 021 613 3333, fax: 021 613 3334, <www.brp.ch>.* Often voted one of the finest hotels in Europe, this 'palace' has been host to famous personalites from around the world since the mid-19th century. Located in Ouchy, on the lakefront. 169 rooms.

Hôtel Angleterre and Résidence $$$$ *place du Port 11, tel: 021 613 3434, fax: 021 613 3435, <www.angleterre-residence.ch>.* Perfectly situated near the shores of Lake Geneva, this modern hotel consists of six buildings, both old and new. Right next to and owned by the Beau-Rivage, guests can use the fitness facilities at its bigger and more expensive neighbour for a small fee. 75 rooms.

Hotel Regina $$$ *rue Grand Saint-Jean 18, tel: 021 320 2441, fax: 021 320 2529, <www.hotel-regina.ch>.* In the old town, in a largely pedestrian area. Affordable rooms and very friendly and helpful staff. 36 rooms.

LEUKERBAD

Lindner Hotels and Alpentherme $$$ *tel: 027 472 1000, fax: 027 472 1001, <www.lindnerhotels.ch>*. Large resort hotel with indoor and outdoor thermal baths and a variety of other wellness options. 135 rooms.

LOCARNO

Hotel Belvedere $$$ *Via ai Monti della Trinità 44, tel: 091 751 0363, fax: 091 751 5239, <www.belvedere-locarno.ch>*. Renovated mansion located on a hill overlooking Locarno and Lake Maggiore. All guest rooms offer views of the lake and most of them come with balconies. 80 rooms.

Hotel Dell'Angelo $ *Piazza Grande, tel: 091 751 8175, fax: 091 751 8256, <www.hotel-dell-angelo.ch>*. Inexpensive, family-run hotel in the centre of Locarno. Friendly, helpful staff. 55 rooms.

LUCERNE

Hotel Krone $$$ *Weinmarkt 12, tel: 041 419 4400, fax: 041 419 4490, <www.bestwestern.ch/kroneluzern>*. A simple, no-frills option overlooking the Weinmarkt square in the old town. Rooms are clean and modern. Good value, especially for the location. 25 rooms.

The Hotel $$$$ *Sempacherstrasse 14, tel: 041 226 8686, fax: 041 226 8690, <www.the-hotel.ch>*. One of Switzerland's most distinctive hotels, this so-called 'deluxe boutique' hotel mixes modern conveniences with a chic atmosphere. Designed by Jean Nouvel, who designed Lucerne's new convention centre. 25 rooms.

Wilden Mann $$$–$$$$ *Bahnhofstrasse 30, tel: 041 210 1666, fax: 041 210 1629, <www.wilden-mann.ch>*. With traditional décor and old-world charm, the Wilden Mann combines seven old townhouses to create one of Lucerne's most famous hotels. The name comes from the 'Wild Man' symbol of medieval folklore and the hotel creates a rustic ambiance befitting an ancient myth. 50 rooms.

LUGANO

Hotel International au Lac $$–$$$ *Via Nassa 68, tel: 091 922 7541, fax: 091 922 7544, <www.hotel-international.ch>.* Operated by the same family since 1906, this reasonably priced hotel is ideally situated in the centre of Lugano and by the lake. Only open Easter–October. 80 rooms.

Principe Leopoldo and Residence $$$$$ *Via Montalbano 5, tel: 091 985 8855, fax: 091 985 8825, <www.leopoldohotel.com>.* Built by Prussian Prince Frederic Leopold, this is one of Lugano's top and most interesting hotels. The rooms and suites are combined into two buildings on Lugano's 'Golden Hill'. Extensive fitness options including two pools and spa. 78 rooms.

Romantik Hotel Ticino $$$$ *Piazza Cioccaro 1, tel: 091 922 7772, fax: 091 923 6278, <www.romantikhotels.com/lugano>.* Close to the lake in the centre of Lugano, this small hotel offers comfortable rooms in a relaxed setting, with a peaceful courtyard. Closed January and first part of February. 18 rooms.

MONTREUX

Eden Palace au Lac $$$–$$$$ *rue du Théâtre 11, tel: 021 966 0800, fax: 021 966 0900, <www.edenpalace.ch>.* Not as luxurious or as expensive as some of its neighbours along the lake in Montreux, but a nonetheless elegant hotel offering great views of Lake Geneva and the Alps. 110 rooms.

MURTEN

Hotel Adler $ *Hauptgasse 45, tel: 026 672 6669, fax: 026 672 6677, <www.adler-hotel.ch>.* Quaint, old, family-run hotel that was completely renovated in 2002 and has a selection of charming, imaginatively decorated rooms named after the famous guests who have stayed here, Goethe and Casanova among them. Unbeatable location in the heart of the old town, a few minutes' stroll from the lake. 24 rooms.

NEUCHÂTEL

La Maison du Prussien $$ *rue des Tunnels 11, tel: 032 730 5454, fax: 032 730 2143, <www.hotel-prussien.ch>*. In an old brewery from the 18th century, this quaint hotel is tucked away among the trees in a natural setting that contains a stream and old mills. A little hard to find, but decent value in an interesting location. 10 rooms.

PONTRESINA

Hotel Müller $$$ *tel: 081 839 3000, fax: 081 839 3030, <www.hotel-mueller.ch>*. Century-old hotel renovated in 2005. Small with bright, modern rooms. Italian restaurant. 18 rooms.

ST-GALLEN

Einstein $$$–$$$$ *Berneggstrasse 2, tel: 071 227 5555, fax: 071 227 5577, <www.einstein.ch>*. Named after a textile manufacturer, the Einstein served as an embroidery factory and a charity among other things before being transformed into a hotel in the early 1980s. Modern, comfortable rooms near the abbey. 113 rooms.

ST MORITZ

Hotel Soldanella $$$–$$$$ *Via Somplaz 17, tel: 081 830 8500, fax: 081 830 8505, <www.hotel-soldanella.ch>*. A nice, affordable option for St Moritz, which has many upscale choices. The Soldanella provides clean, modern rooms and a wellness centre for relaxation. Some rooms come with fantastic views of the Engadine mountains. 35 rooms. Closed several months during late spring and autumn.

Suvretta House $$$$–$$$$$ *Via Chasellas 1, tel: 081 836 3636, fax: 081 836 3737, <www.suvrettahouse.ch>*. One of St Moritz's grand hotels, the Suvretta's location is undeniably special. The hotel has a park-like setting and their own ski-lift is nearby, so outdoor activities are easily accessible. They even have their own ski school, curling surface and skating rink. 189 rooms. Closed several months during late spring and autumn.

SCHAFFHAUSEN

Rheinhotel Fischerzunft $$$ *Rheinquai 8, tel: 052 632 0505, fax: 052 632 0513, <www.fischerzunft.ch>.* A small Relais and Chateaux inn located on the Rhine river. Some rooms have views of the Rhine. Popular restaurant. 10 rooms.

SOLOTHURN

Hotel Krone $$$ *Hauptgasse 64, tel: 032 626 4444, fax: 032 626 4445, <www.diekrone.ch>.* A historic hotel that claims to be Switzerland's second oldest. Also claims Napoleon and Josephine as past guests, as well as Sophia Loren. Décor combines antiques with modern amenities. 42 rooms.

WENGEN

Hotel Caprice $$$$ *tel: 033 856 0606, fax: 033 856 0607, <www. caprice-wengen.ch>.* A new building (1989) that blends into the alpine scenery outside and provides modern rooms and conveniences on the inside. Located near the town centre and close to the slopes. Closed several months in spring and autumn. 18 rooms.

ZERMATT

Coeur des Alpes $$$–$$$$ *tel: 027 966 4080, fax: 027 966 4081, <www.coeurdesalpes.ch>.* A combination of Swiss chalet (exposed wood beams) and modern décor (with a glass-floor lounge that looks down into the spa). Small, with seven suites and six double rooms. Consider the Penthouse Suite, which has magnificent views of the Matterhorn.

Hotel Daniela $$ *tel: 027 966 7700, fax: 027 966 7777, <www. hoteldaniela.ch>.* An inexpensive option that is great value compared to the usually higher-priced Zermatt hotels and inns. Guests are welcome to use the wellness centre at its sister hotel, the Julen (<www.julen.ch>), which is a little more expensive and just a short walk away. 24 rooms.

The Omnia $$$$$ *tel: 027 966 7171, <www.the-omnia.com>*. A brand new mountain-lodge-style hotel with all modern conveniences, situated just above Zermatt. Pool, outdoor Jacuzzi, and other wellness options.

ZURICH

Greulich Hotel $$ *Herman-Greulich-Strasse 56, tel: 043 243 4243, <www.greulich.ch>*. A small hotel in a quiet neighbourhood with a peaceful inner courtyard and modern design. Just outside the city centre. 18 rooms.

Hotel Adler $$ *Rosengasse 10, tel: 044 266 9696, fax: 044 266 9669, <www.hotel-adler.ch>*. Renovated hotel with basic, modern rooms. Located on the right bank, in the heart of the old town. Great value and location for exploring Zurich. Popular restaurant, Swiss Chuchi, serves traditional Swiss fare. 52 rooms.

Hotel Hirschen $$ *Niederdorfstrasse 13, tel: 043 268 3333, fax: 043 268 3334, <www.hirschen-zuerich.ch>*. Affordable hotel with modern, comfortable rooms just steps away from the Limmat river on the right bank. The walls of the famous wine cellar, Weinschenke, date back to the 16th century. 27 rooms.

Romantik Hotel Florhof $$$$ *Florhofgasse 4, tel: 044 250 2626, fax: 044 250 2627, <www.florhof.ch>*. Situated on a quiet street on the right bank of the lake, this former merchant's house has been transformed into a quaint boutique hotel with an excellent restaurant. Consider the junior suites if you desire a little more space. 33 rooms.

Widder Hotel $$$$$ *Rennweg 7, tel: 044 224 2526, fax: 044 224 2424, <www.widderhotel.ch>*. One of Zurich's finest and most famous hotels, the Widder comprises no less than eight interconnected historic townhouses in the heart of Zurich. Each building was remodelled in a unique fashion and the rooms are decorated individually as well, so that no two are alike. Seven suites available, some with a rooftop terrace. 49 rooms.

Recommended Restaurants

Many restaurants in Switzerland offer daily lunch specials; some will offer two or three each day. These are usually a great bargain, ranging from 15–30 Swiss francs. Many restaurants will offer dinner menus which can also be good value. Some restaurants close on Sundays and during the month of August, when much of the country is on holiday. A tip is usually included, but it is customary to add an additional amount for exceptional service (5 percent). In most of the resort towns, restaurants will be found in the many hotels.

The following price guide indicates the approximate cost of a meal for two, excluding drinks.

$$$$	over CHF100
$$$	CHF75–100
$$	CHF50–75
$	below CHF50

BASEL

Der Vierte König $$ *Blumenrain 20, tel: 061 261 5442*. Overlooking the Rhine, this restaurant/wine bar has a diverse menu with delicious soups and pastas. But wine is the focus here – and as part of the décor as bottles line the walls. The entrance is off Blumenrain as the front door faces the Rhine. Closed Sunday.

Stucki Bruderholz $$$$ *Bruderholzallee 42, tel: 061 361 8222, <www.stucki-bruderholz.ch>*. Probably Basel's most famous restaurant and one of the best in Switzerland. French cuisine that offers a changing, seasonal menu which might include Bresse chicken, Chamois or white truffles from Alba. Outdoor dining in the garden in summer. Closed Sunday and Monday.

Zum Braunen Mutz $$–$$ *Barfüsserplatz 10, tel: 061 261 3369, <www.brauner-mutz-basel.ch>*. Located on the busy Barfüsserplatz in the centre of Basel, Zum Braunen Mutz offers two restaurants under one roof. A casual brasserie on the ground level with outdoor terrace (great place to people watch while grabbing lunch) serving French, German and Italian specialities. More formal – and expensive – dining upstairs in the gourmet restaurant.

BERN

Altes Tramdepot $–$$ *Grosser Muristalden 6, tel: 031 368 1415, <www.altestramdepot.ch>*. In an old tram hall, right by the Bear Pit. Brewery with typical beer-hall cuisine, such as the house speciality, Bavarian sausages with mustard and pretzel. During warmer months, there is a terrace that overlooks the city. Great place to grab lunch while visiting the bears.

Kornhauskeller $$–$$$ *Kornhausplatz 18, tel: 031 327 7272*. In an old corn cellar, this vast underground restaurant was renovated to keep much of the original detail and walls of the original structure. A dark, but vibrant eatery resulted that focuses on Italian cuisine. A bistro/café above ground offers lighter fare and outdoor seating during the summer.

Wein und Sein $$$ *Münstergasse 50, tel: 031 311 9844, <www. weinundsein.ch>*. Located in a cellar under Bern's famous arcades. Enter through the cellar doors to this small restaurant where every night you have but one option: the menu that is designed for that day. Reservations required. Closed Sunday and Monday.

CHUR

Duc de Rohan $$ *Masanserstrasse 44, tel: 081 252 1022*. One of the region's best restaurants with a pleasant outdoor terrace and changing daily menu.

DAVOS

Bistro Gentiana et Café des Artistes $$–$$$ *Promenade 53, tel: 081 413 5649, <www.gentiana.ch>*. In Davos-Platz, a trendy bistro with several fondue varieties and also a selection of snail dishes. Closed Wednesdays during the summer.

GENEVA

Café des Négociants $$$–$$$$ *rue de la Filature 29, tel: 022 300 3130, <www.negociants.ch>*. Situated just outside Geneva, but just a short tram-ride away, in the popular suburb of Carouge. One of many excellent dining options in Carouge. Extensive wine selection. Larger groups can eat at a big table in the wine cellar. Closed Saturday and Sunday.

Demi Lune $ *rue Etienne Dumont 3, tel: 022 312 1290, <www.demi lune.ch>*. With a swank, lounge feel, this small café is popular for a late-night cocktail or glass of wine, but also has an eclectic menu ranging from burgers and sandwiches to different tapas to chicken tandoori. Saturday and Sunday open evenings only.

L'Auberge d'Hermance $$$$ *rue du Midi 12, Hermance, tel: 022 751 1368, <www.hotel-hermance.ch>*. Nestling on a narrow street in the quaint village of Hermance (just before the French border along the left bank). Enchanting French restaurant with vine-covered terrace in the summer. Also a small inn with six rooms.

Les Armures $$–$$$ *rue du Puits-St-Pierre 1, tel: 022 310 3442, <www.hotel-les-armures.ch>*. Housed in the famous Hotel Les Armures in the heart of the old town. Serving some of the best fondue in Geneva as well as other traditional Swiss cuisine.

GRUYÈRES

Le Chalet $–$$ *tel: 026 921 2154, <www.chalet-gruyeres.ch>*. Great place for a quintessential, traditional Swiss dining experience from the chalet exterior to the all-wood interior to the heavy, cheese-and-meat-focused cuisine. Excellent *raclette* and fondue. As does much of Gruyères, caters to tourists.

GSTAAD

Chesery $$$$ *Lauenenstrasse, tel: 033 744 2451*. Chef Robert Speth offers an ever-changing menu focusing on the seasons. One of the finest restaurants in the Bernese Oberland, and Switzerland. Closed Monday and usually in late spring and late autumn.

INTERLAKEN

Schuh $$ *Höheweg 56, tel: 033 822 9441, <www.schuh-interlaken. ch>.* Especially popular in summer because diners can sit on the large terrace, from where there are superb views of the Jungfrau. Food is decent, if not spectacular, and it's certainly eclectic, with a European, Chinese and Thai menu.

LAUSANNE

Louis $$–$$$ *place de l'Europe 9, tel: 021 213 0300.* A combination of *vinotheque*, bistro and gourmet restaurant. The wine bar and bistro provide a relaxed atmosphere for grabbing a glass of wine or having a light lunch, with excellent *plat du jour* options. For dinner, you can dine in the bistro or the more formal, gourmet restaurant upstairs.

Philippe Rochat $$$$ *rue d'Yverdon 1, Crissier, tel: 021 634 0505, <www.philippe-rochat.ch>.* Usually considered the best restaurant in Switzerland, and thus one of the world's best, Philippe Rochat took over this Swiss institution from Fredy Girardet (former name) and has maintained its status among the culinary elite. Make reservations well in advance. Closed Sunday and Monday.

LOCARNO

Ristorante Cittadella $$–$$$ *Via Cittadella 18, tel: 091 751 5885, <www.cittadella.ch>.* A trattoria downstairs and a more formal restaurant upstairs specializing in fish and seafood. Located in the Old Town. Also is a small hotel. Closed Mondays.

LUCERNE

Old Swiss House $$$$ *Löwenplatz 4, tel: 041 410 6171, <www. oldswisshouse.ch>.* A Lucerne staple for decades. The interior is decorated with antiques and is heavy on wood, befitting a Swiss chalet. Traditional cuisine. Try the house speciality, *wienerschnitzel*. Closed Monday.

Schiff $–$$ *Unter der Egg 8, tel: 041 418 5252, <www.hotel-schiff-luzern.ch>*. Serves decent traditional Swiss cuisine mainly to tourists who come for the ideal location, a large terrace right on the river with a view of the Kapellbrücke.

LUGANO

Al Portone $$$ *Viale Cassarate 3, tel: 091 923 5511, <www.ristorante alportone.ch>*. Creative Italian cuisine, blending traditional dishes with a modern flair. Closed Sunday and Monday and in August.

Tinera $ *Via dei Gorini 2, tel: 091 923 5219*. Italian grotto atmosphere in a basement restaurant. Very casual with good-value pasta dishes and other Italian specialities. Closed Sunday and Monday, and in August.

NEUCHÂTEL

Maison des Halles $$ *rue du Trésor 4, tel: 032 724 3141, <www. maisondeshalles.ch>*. A casual café with outdoor terrace, and a gourmet restaurant (for groups of 10 or more only), combine in a 16th-century building to give two fine dining options.

ST-GALLEN

Jägerhof $$$$ *Brühlbleichestrasse 11, tel: 071 245 5022, <www. jaegerhof.ch>*. Highly awarded restaurant that uses fresh market produce to create diverse seasonal menus. Several rooms also available for accommodation.

ST MORITZ

Engiadina $–$$ *Piazza da Scuola 2, tel: 081 833 3265*. A good place for a reasonably priced Swiss meal. The food is straightforward and hearty: fondues, carpaccio, steak. Located in the heart of St Moritz Dorf. Closed Sunday and in November.

SCHAFFHAUSEN

Gerberstrube $$$ *Bachstrasse 8, tel: 052 625 2155*. Popular Italian restaurant serving traditional cuisine and some international specialities. Closed Sunday and Monday.

ZERMATT

Schäferstübli $$ *in Romantik Hotel Julen, tel: 027 966 7600, <www.julen.ch>*. Traditional Valais and Swiss specialities are served, including fondues and *raclette*. The Julen also has a more upscale restaurant with an international menu.

ZURICH

Hiltl $ *Sihlstrasse 28, tel: 044 227 7000, <www.hiltl.ch>*. The oldest vegetarian restaurant in Europe, Hiltl has been a Zurich landmark for more than 100 years. The menu encompasses a multitude of different salads, pastas, curries and fruit juices, among other choices.

Kronenhalle $$$–$$$$ *Rämistrasse 4, tel: 044 262 9900, <www.kronenhalle.com>*. One of Zurich's most popular restaurants. Serves excellent French international cuisine in a traditional French brasserie atmosphere.

Rosaly's $$ *Freieckgasse 7, tel: 044 261 4430, <www.rosalys.ch>*. A popular bar and restaurant that combines produce of the season with a Californian flair. Diverse soups and salads are offered here, along with some creative daily specials. Live music some Saturdays.

Zeughauskeller $$ *Bahnhofstrasse 28A, tel: 044 211 2690, <www.zeughauskeller.ch>*. Down the Bahnhofstrasse at the Paradeplatz, this is a perfect place to tuck into some traditional Swiss fare in a 15th-century building that can accommodate 240 diners. Patrons fill the huge, long tables, often sitting with complete strangers.

INDEX

Berlitz pocket guide

Switzerland

Sixth Edition 2008

Written by Ken Bernstein
Updated by David Dalton
Series Editor: Tony Halliday

Printed in Singapore by Insight Print Services (Pte) Ltd, 38 Joo Koon Road, Singapore 628990. Tel: (65) 6865-1600. Fax: (65) 6861-6438

Berlitz Trademark Reg. U.S. Patent Office and other countries. Marca Registrada

Photography credits
Jerry Dennis 15, 22, 26, 27, 29, 33, 41, 48, 77, 84, 85, 86, 90, 106, 111, 124, 138, 145; swiss-image.ch 6, 7, 12, 30, 37, 39, 42, 55, 61, 63, 71, 72, 75, 78, 92, 97, 98, 104, 120, 123, 137, 141, 142, 147; BLS/swiss-image.ch 11, 58; ST/swiss-image.ch 9, 20, 34, 35, 40, 44, 46, 53, 70, 79, 83, 100, 103, 107, 109, 112, 115, 118, 127, 128, 131, 132; Bill Wassman 51, 65, 67, 73, 80, 89, 94, 96, 113, 117; Topham Picturepoint 16; Punktum Bildarchiv: Schweizerisches Landesmuseum Zürich 17.

Cover picture: Jon Arnold/Jon Arnold Images

Contact us

At Berlitz we strive to keep our guides as accurate and up to date as possible, but if you find anything that has changed, or if you have any suggestions on ways to improve this guide, then we would be delighted to hear from you.

Berlitz Publishing, PO Box 7910, London SE1 1WE, England.
fax: (44) 20 7403 0290
email: berlitz@apaguide.co.uk
www.berlitzpublishing.co.uk